# MEDIAEVAL SOURCES
# IN TRANSLATION

## 32

# St. Thomas Aquinas

# FAITH, REASON AND THEOLOGY

Questions I-IV of his Commentary
on the *De Trinitate* of Boethius
translated with Introduction
and Notes

*by*

ARMAND MAURER

PONTIFICAL INSTITUTE
OF MEDIAEVAL STUDIES

**Canadian Cataloguing in Publication Data**

Thomas, Aquinas, Saint, 1225?-1274
  Faith, reason and theology

(Mediaeval sources in translation; 32)
Translated from: Expositio super librum Boethii De trinitate.
Biblioigraphy: p.
Indluces index.
ISBN 0-88844-282-3

1. Boethius, d. 524. De Trinitate. 2. Trinity — Early works to 1800. I. Maurer,
Armand A. (Armand Augustine), 1915-    . II. Pontifical Institute of
Mediaeval Studies. III. Title. IV. Series.

BT110.T4613 1987            231'.044            C87-094669-2

© 1987 by

Pontifical Institute of Mediaeval Studies
59 Queen's Park Crescent East
Toronto, Ontario, Canada   M5S 2C4
Printed in Canada by University of Toronto Press Incorporated

# Contents

# Abbreviations

CCL　*Corpus Christianorum, series latina. Continuatio mediaevalis*
　　　(Turnhout, 1951 — )

CSEL　*Corpus scriptorum ecclesiasticorum latinorum*, ed. G. Schepps
　　　and S. Brandt (Vienna, 1866-1913).

PG　*Patrologia graeco-latina*, ed. J.-P. Migne (Paris, 1844-1864;
　　　repr. Turnhout, 1958-72).

PL　*Patrologia latina*, as above.

# Translator's Introduction

## A. DATE AND COMPOSITION OF THE COMMENTARY

The commentary on the *De Trinitate* of Boethius is one of Thomas Aquinas' earliest theological works. He composed it about 1255-1259, during the beginning of his tenure as Regent Master at the University of Paris.[1] The circumstances of his writing a commentary on the treatise of Boethius—a practice long out of fashion—are unknown. The plausible suggestion has been made that it is the product of his teaching at the Dominican priory of St. Jacques in Paris before he began teaching as a Master of Theology at the university. In the spring of 1256 he received his licence to teach in the Faculty of Theology, but owing to a dispute between the secular and religious masters the university did not admit him as a master with full teaching rights until the fall of that year. During the half year of waiting he may have taught at the Dominican priory, and one of the results of this teaching may have been the exposition of Boethius' *De Trinitate*. By this time he had already taught the *Sentences* of Peter Lombard as Bachelor of the Sentences (1252-1256). As he took up his duties as a master at the university in the fall of 1256, teaching the prescribed texts of the Bible, he would have discontinued his commentary on the *De Trinitate*—a work that was not on the university curriculum. This would explain why he left the commentary unfinished, lecturing only on Boethius' prologue, chapter 1 and a part of chapter 2.[2] It

---

[1] See B. Decker, *Sancti Thomae de Aquino. Expositio super librum Boethii De Trinitate*, Prol., p. 44. M.-D. Chenu proposes the date 1256 in "La date du commentaire de S. Thomas sur le *De Trinitate* de Boèce," *Revue des sciences philosophiques et théologiques* 30 (1941-42) 432-434. J. Weisheipl places it between 1253 and 1258 in *Friar Thomas d'Aquino. His Life, Thought, and Work*, 2nd ed., pp. 381-382, 469.

[2] See S. Neumann, *Gegenstand und Methode der theoretischen Wissenschaften nach Thomas von Aquin*, p. 6; L. Elders, *Faith and Science*, pp. 19-20.

was his intention, however, to continue the commentary.[3] Whatever the reason for his failing to do so, the work was terminated by 1258 or 1259. A large portion of it is extant in his own "illegible" handwriting, with his corrections and additions.[4]

Thomas uses both the literal and question form of commentary in his treatment of the *De Trinitate*. He begins with a general introduction to the work, then gives a brief sentence by sentence explanation of a section of the Boethian text, beginning with the prologue. He then selects certain problems arising from the text and treats them in the form of extended questions. These questions are six in number, each subdivided into four articles. Topics of the questions and articles are far-ranging, reflecting problems in theology and philosophy that were currently being debated. All of them were intended to introduce the audience or reader to the theology of the Trinity, which is the main subject of the treatise of Boethius. The articles reveal the youthful Thomas as already a true master of his subject, well versed in sacred Scripture, the Fathers of the Church, and what was known of the philosophers of antiquity, but carrying forward their teachings in a profound and creative way.

Despite the wide variety of themes debated in these questions, they have a unity in the fact that they all contribute to an understanding of the nature of theology, especially the theology of the Trinity. Questions 1-3 treat of the capacities and limitations of human knowledge when its object is God. They defend a "scientific" knowledge of God in which faith plays the principal part and human reason, particularly in the form of philosophy, is cast in an ancillary role. Question 4, following the text of Boethius, takes up an entirely different problem: the factors relating to the cause of plurality. Thomas here elucidates the basis for plurality and the principle of individuation— themes that are central for the theology of the Trinity. Questions 5-6 are devoted to the division of the theoretical sciences and their respective methods. The main purpose of these questions is to locate the theology handed down in sacred Scripture, as distinct from philosophical theology or metaphysics, among the theoretical sciences

---

[3] See *In Boeth. de Trin.*, Q. 6, a. 3, ed. Decker, p. 222.19, trans. A. Maurer, *The Division and Methods of the Sciences*, p. 86.

[4] See Decker, ibid., p. 1. The autograph extends from the end of Q. 3, a. 2 to the end of the opuscule.

and to clarify its method. Over thirty years ago I translated these questions with the title: *St. Thomas Aquinas. The Division and Methods of the Sciences.*[5] The present translation of Questions 1-4 completes the translation of Thomas' commentary.

## B. THEOLOGY

In Questions 1-3 Thomas lays down the principles for a reform of theology that he carried out principally in his two *Summae.*[6] Theology for him, as for the Fathers of the Church, was a reflection on the mysteries of faith in order to gain an understanding of what he believed, but this reflection and understanding was now to take the form of a science, or better, a wisdom, modelled as closely as possible on the Aristotelian notion of a science, as described in

---

[5] *St. Thomas Aquinas. The Division and Methods of the Sciences.* Questions v and vi of his Commentary on the *De Trinitate* of Boethius, translated with Introduction and Notes. 1st ed. Toronto, 1953; 4th ed. Toronto, 1986.

[6] For Thomas' notion of theology and its place in history, see M.-D. Chenu, *La théologie comme science au XIIIᵉ siècle*; idem, *Faith and Theology*; idem, *Toward Understanding Saint Thomas*; idem *Is Theology a Science?* Y. Congar, *Thomas d'Aquin: sa vision de théologie et de l'Église*; idem, *A History of Theology*, pp. 91-114. M. Grabmann, *Die theologische Erkenntnis- und Einleitungslehre des hl. Thomas von Aquin auf Grund seiner Schrift "In Boethium de Trinitate" im Zusammenhang der Scholastik des 13. und beginnenden 14. Jahrhunderts dargestellt.*

In the *Summa theologiae* the term "theology" is seldom used. The preferred term in this work is *sacra doctrina* (sacred teaching); in the commentary on Boethius it is *scientia divina* (divine science). For Thomas, sacred doctrine is the teaching revealed by God in sacred Scripture. More generally, it embraces "whatever pertains to the Christian religion," (*Summa*, prol.). In one of its parts it has the character of a science, inasmuch as necessary consequences are drawn from revealed teachings. Included in the science of theology are also all that the theologian borrows from philosophy and the secular sciences in order to elucidate the meaning of revealed doctrines.

For Thomas' notion of *sacra doctrina*, see G. F. Van Ackeren, *Sacra Doctrina. The Subject of the First Question of the Summa Theologica of St. Thomas Aquinas.* E. Gilson, *Elements of Christian Philosophy*, pp. 22-42. Y. Congar, *A History of Theology*, pp. 92-96. J. Weisheipl, "The Meaning of *Sacra Doctrina* in *Summa Theologiae* I, q. 1," *The Thomist* 38 (1974), 49-80.

Aristotle's *Posterior Analytics*.[7] According to Aristotle, every science has its own subject, whose attributes and causes are demonstrated in the light of certain basic principles. Science in this broad sense is not only knowledge of facts but *reasoned* knowledge. Applying this notion to theology, Thomas shows that the subject of theology is God, for the main effort of the theologian is to know him. As the word indicates, theology (*theologia*) is a disquisition about God. His immediate predecessors and contemporaries proposed other subjects for theology, for example "things and signs" (Peter Lombard), the works of salvation (Hugh of St. Victor), or the whole Christ, both head and members, that is, the Church, (Robert Kilwardby).[8] While conceding that theology deals with all of these, Thomas insisted that only God can be the subject of theology, for "in sacred doctrine all things are treated under the aspect of God, either because they are God himself, or because they refer to God as to their beginning and end."[9]

---

[7] For Aristotle's notion of science see *Post. Anal.* 1.2-14, (71b8-79a33). W. Wallace, *Causality and Scientific Explanation*, 1:11-18. J. Owens, "The Aristotelian Conception of the Sciences," *Aristotle. The Collected Papers of Joseph Owens*, pp. 23-34.

[8] See *Summa theol.* 1.1.7. References to medieval theologians holding these views on the subject of theology are found in the notes to the Gilby edition of the *Summa* 1: 2-27.

[9] *Summa theol.* ibid. Some modern theologians propose human existence as the subject of theology. See C. J. Peter, "A Shift to the Human Subject in Roman Catholic Theology," *Communio* 6.1 (1979) 56: "As I shall use the term, Christian theology is a methodical effort to understand human existence—an effort made in dependence on Christian Faith." Without denying that God is the formal object of theology, some theologians speak of a "transcendental anthropological dimension of theology" because theology is theology of human salvation (*Heilstheologie*), and this salvation is the triune God. See C. Moeller, "Renewal of the Doctrine of Man," *Theology of Renewal* 2: 422-424. See also K. Rahner, "Theology and Anthropology," *Theological Investigations* 9:28-45; idem, "Theology," *Sacramentum Mundi* 6: 233-246; idem, *Grundsätzliche Überlegungen zur Anthropologie und Protologie im Rahmen der Theologie. Mysterium Salutis* 2. *Die Heilsgeschichte vor Christus*, pp. 406-420. This approach to theology uses a transcendental method that owes more to Kant and the German idealists than to Thomas Aquinas.

Liberation theologians conceive theology as a critical reflection on praxis, that is, real charity, action and commitment to the service of men. Theology for them springs from and reflects on this definite praxis. See Gustavo Gutierrez, *A Theology of Liberation: History, Politics and Salvation*, pp. 5-13. For Aquinas, theology is not merely theoretical, unengaged with human salvation and liberation, but "it is

Besides a subject, every science has principles or starting-points which illuminate everything else in the science. The starting-point of our human path to God is the sensible world. The metaphysician adopts this empirical starting-point, finding in the data of the sensible world intelligible traces of God which lead him to elaborate a science of God. Philosophical theology is truly a divine science, but a nobler one is possible which takes its principles from the articles of faith. [10]

The obvious objection is that the theologian does not know his principles, but only believes them. He accepts them on the authority of God who reveals them in sacred Scripture. Can there be a science in which faith plays such an important role? Thomas points out that even in the realm of the purely human sciences faith and authority can play a part. There are sciences that accept principles or basic truths from other sciences. These are called subalternated sciences because in a sense they come under the sciences from which they borrow principles. For example, the science of medicine accepts on the testimony of the physicist many facts about the nature of matter. The physicist himself uses mathematical principles that are either self evident or proved only in mathematics. [11]

On the analogy of these subalternated sciences Thomas conceives theology as a science whose principles are believed on the authority of God who reveals them in sacred Scripture. [12] This is a use of the Aristotelian notion of science, but one that Aristotle himself would not have recognized. In fact, Thomas has transposed the notion of science to a new and unexpected level. The Aristotelian subalternated science proceeds from principles of a higher science, but they are known by the natural light of reason in the higher science, whereas theology proceeds from principles transcending the whole order of natural reason. Thus "it enjoys the unique privilege of proceeding

---

more speculative than practical, because it is more concerned with divine realities than with human acts." *Summa theol.* 1.1.4.

[10] For the two meanings of theology, see Q. 2, a. 2, below, pp. 41-42, and Q. 5, a. 4, ed. Decker, p. 195.6-27, trans. Maurer, pp. 52-53.

[11] Ibid., Q. 2, a. 2, Reply to 5, below, p. 44. See Q. 5, a. 1, Reply to 5, ed. Decker, pp. 170-171, trans. Maurer, pp. 21-22.

[12] Ibid., Q. 2, a. 2, Reply to 7, below, p. 44. In his commentary on the *Sentences* Thomas says that theology is, *as it were* (*quasi*), subalternated to the divine knowledge. *Sent.* Prol. 1.3, sol. 2; ed. Mandonnet, 1:14.

from principles made known, by revelation, in the light of the science that God has of Himself and of all other beings."[13] As a result, sacred doctrine (*sacra doctrina*) bears, as it were, the stamp of God's own knowledge.[14]

Though theology uses the authority of divine revelation to establish its principles, it does not become a science unless it investigates the contents of revelation by means of reason. Some of the Fathers of the Church, like Ambrose and Hilary, Thomas remarks, had recourse only to the method of authority. Others, such as Augustine and Boethius, combined both authority and reason.[15] In a quodlibetal question written toward the end of his career (1271), Thomas distinguishes between two kinds of theological disputes. One aims to dispel any doubt about the fact of the matter (*an ita sit*), and for this the theologian mainly uses authority. For example, in disputing with Jews he will advance the authority of the Old Testament; in his discussions with Manichees, who refuse to accept this Testament, he must appeal only to the New Testament. If the disputant will accept no authority, the theologian must try to convince his opponent by rational arguments. The other kind of dispute is the "magistral disputation used in the schools" (*quaedam vero disputatio est magistralis in scholis*). Its purpose is to instruct the hearers and lead them to the truth, relying on reasoning that probes its very depths. It shows the hearers not only that such and such is true, but *how* it is true (*quomodo sit verum quod dicitur*). The hearers then acquire science and understanding.[16]

Thomas himself made use of both theological methods. He often cities authorities, not only in his voluminous scriptural commentaries, but also in his works that have the form of disputation. As for reasoning and explanation, these are an integral part of his commentaries on Scripture, but they are more prominent in his magistral disputations

---

[13] E. Gilson, *Elements of Christian Philosophy*, p. 29. In his actual practice of theology Thomas does not merely use the deductive method, deducing conclusions from revealed premises. He also employs experience and manifold modes of reasoning (as Aristotle himself did in his science), but always in the light of revelation. See C. Ernst, "Theological Methodology," *Sacramentum Mundi* 6:222.

[14] See, Q. 3, a. 1, Reply to 4, below, p. 69; *Summa theol.*, 1.1.3, ad 2.

[15] See St. Thomas' Introduction, below, pp. 5-6.

[16] St. Thomas, *Quodlibet* 4, Q. 9, a. 18.

(the Disputed and Quodlibetal Questions), his commentaries on the *Sentences* of Peter Lombard and the *De Trinitate* of Boethius, and his two *Summae*. It is especially in these later works that theology rises to the level of a science.[17]

## C. USE OF PHILOSOPHY IN THEOLOGY

One of Thomas' most forceful defences of the use of philosophy in theology is contained in the present work, Question Two, Article Three. Not all his contemporaries shared his appreciation of the value of philosophy, particularly that of Aristotle, in the work of theology. Albert the Great refers to "some who in their complete ignorance want to oppose the use of philosophy. This is especially true among the Dominicans, where no one stands up to contradict them. Like brute animals they blaspheme against things they do not understand."[18] Thomas inherited his teacher's robust confidence in the value of human reason and its achievements in the arts and philosophy, and he staunchly defended their use in theology. He himself was open to the influence of Aristotle and his Muslim commentators, as well as to elements in the Neoplatonic tradition handed down by Augustine, Boethius and the Pseudo-Dionysius. But when necessary he corrected and modified everything he borrowed from his predecessors in the creation of his own philosophy.[19]

Philosophy and theology are clearly distinct for Aquinas, for philosophy depends on the natural light of reason and theology on the

---

[17] See M. Grabmann, *Die theol. Erkenntnis- und Einleitungslehre des hl. Thomas von Aquin...*, pp. 162-163. This is not to belittle the importance of Thomas' commentaries on Scripture. As a master of theology his official teaching consisted in explaining the text of Scripture. For his principles of scriptural exegesis, see B. Smalley, *The Study of the Bible in the Middle Ages*; H. de Lubac, *Exégèse médiévale. Les quatre sens de l'Écriture*, 2e partie, 2: 272-302.

[18] Albert the Great, *In opera B. Dionysii Areopagitae*, Ep. 7, n. 2B, ed. Borgnet 14: 910. See J. Weisheipl, *Friar Thomas d'Aquino*, p. 43. For the cautionary attitude of some 13th century theologians and ecclesiastical authorities at Paris toward the newly discovered philosophies of Aristotle and the Muslim philosophies, see E. Gilson, *History of Christian Philosophy in the Middle Ages*, pp. 244-246.

[19] See E. Gilson, *The Christian Philosophy of St. Thomas*; idem, *Elements of Christian Philosophy*.

light of faith. Since both lights come from the same God, philosophy and theology cannot contradict each other. Rather, they are related like the gifts of nature and grace. Grace does not destroy nature but perfects it. Similarly, the light of faith does not do away with the light of reason, but it reveals truths beyond the reach of reason itself. Reason, for its part, can come to the aid of faith in various ways. For example, it can establish certain preambles of faith, such as the existence and unity of God, and it can prove many truths about creatures which faith presupposes. Reason can also use philosophy to refute doctrines contrary to the faith, by showing either that they are completely in error or at least that they have not been demonstratively proven. Philosophy can also throw light on the contents of faith by bringing analogies to bear upon them, as Augustine drew many analogies from philosophy to throw light on the Trinity.[20]

Useful as philosophy may be to the theologian, it also poses dangers for him. He must be wary lest he introduce into his theology erroneous philosophical doctrines contrary to the faith. Thomas cites Origen as an example of one who made this mistake. He thought Origen erred, among other matters, in his teaching on the Word of God and in his angelology.[21] Another mistake the theologian can make is to fall into rationalism, believing only what reason can establish and denying the transcendence of faith over reason. He would try to bring the contents of faith within the bounds of philosophy, whereas he should do just the opposite and bring philosophy within the bounds of faith. Scripture itself is Thomas' warrant for the inclusion of philosophy in theology. St. Paul tells the Corinthians: "We...take every thought captive to obey Christ."[22] As Thomas points out, this had been the program of Augustine in his treatise *On Christian Teaching*. Whatever truths the philosophers have discovered and that are in agreement with our faith, we should not be afraid to incorporate in Christian doctrine.[23] To the objection that this would be diluting the wine of theology with the water of secular wisdom, Thomas astutely replies that "those who use the works of the philosophers

---

[20] See Q. 2, a.3, below, p. 49.

[21] Ibid.

[22] 2 Cor. 10:5. See E. Gilson, "The Intelligence in the Service of Christ the King," *A Gilson Reader*, ed. A. C. Pegis, pp. 31-48.

[23] See St. Thomas, *In I Cor.* 1, lect. 3, ed. Cai 2, p. 308, n. 32; *In Tit.* 1, lect. 3, ed. Cai 1, p. 240, n. 43.

in sacred doctrine, by bringing them into the service of faith, do not mix water with wine, but rather change water into wine."[24]

Few lines in the works of Aquinas reveal more vividly his conception of theology and its relation to philosophy and secular knowledge in general.[25] If we want to see the realization of that conception we have only to open his *Summa theologiae*. In this compendium of theology everything is theological, even the philosophical reasoning that makes up such a large part of it. The water of philosophy and the other secular disciplines it contains has been changed into the wine of theology. That is why we cannot extract from the *Summa* its philosophical parts and treat them as pure philosophy. Everything in the *Summa* is shaped and directed to theological ends. It is considered under the formal object of theology, which is divine revelation, and therefore it belongs to the science of theology.[26]

## D.   DIVINE ILLUMINATION

If the theologian places human intelligence at the service of God in the interpretation of his word, he should give full recognition to the nature and efficacy of that intelligence. Only an intelligence whose nature it is to know the truth is a worthy handmaiden of theology. The dignity and integrity of the human mind is the theme of the first article in the present work (Q 1, a. 1).[27] The question under dispute is whether the mind needs a new illumination by the divine light in order to know the truth. In Thomas' day there were many of the

[24] See Q. 2, a. 3, obj. 5 and reply, below, pp. 46, 50. Bonaventure later took up the metaphor and warned that the water of philosophy is not to be mixed with the wine of Scripture in such a way that the wine becomes water—which would be the worst of miracles! Following the action of Christ, the theologian should turn the water of philosophy into the wine of Scripture. See St. Bonaventure, *Collationes in Hexaëmeron* 19, n. 14, ed. Quaracchi, 5:422. See J. F. Quinn, *The Historical Constitution of St. Bonaventure's Philosophy*, p. 815.

[25] "Thus can theological wisdom, imprinted in the mind of the theologian as the seal of God's knowing, include the totality of human knowledge in its transcendent unity." E. Gilson, *The Philosopher and Theology*, p. 101.

[26] See *Summa theol.* 1.1.3. See also E. Gilson, *Elements of Christian Philosophy*, pp. 30-35. A. C. Pegis, *St. Thomas and Philosophy*, pp. 30-46.

[27] For an historical analysis of this article, see L. Elders, *Faith and Science*, pp. 26-30.

opinion that the mind by itself has insufficient power to do so; for this it needs a special or quasi special illumination by God.

The notion of knowledge by divine illumination goes back to Augustine and his Neoplatonic sources. In his view the mind knows the truth within certain limits, but truth itself, being eternal and immutable, transcends the created and changeable human mind. Hence, if the mind is to know the truth it must be illumined by the eternal and immutable ideas in the mind of God.[28] When the philosophy of Avicenna became known in the thirteenth century, it reinforced the Augustinian doctrine of illumination by teaching that the active intellect, which causes knowledge, exists outside the human soul and illuminates all souls in common, somewhat as the sun enlightens our eyes and enables us to see. A blending of the Augustinian and Avicennian doctrines of illumination strongly appealed to many philosophers in the thirteenth century as the best explanation of human knowledge.[29]

In the spirit of Augustine, William of Auvergne (d. 1249) contended that the light whereby the soul knows is God himself. The creator himself, he argued, is "the book proper and natural to the human intellect," in which the mind reads the primary rules of truth and morality.[30] Bonaventure (d. 1274) did not deny to the mind its own created light of knowing, but he regarded this light as insufficient to judge with certitude about anything without the help of the uncreated light of God.[31]

Thomas readily agreed with Augustine that the mind is illumined by God, but he distinguished more clearly than his predecessors between two forms of illumination, one natural and the other supernatural. The first is the light itself of the human mind, which he

---

[28] See St. Augustine, *Soliloquies* 1.6.12, PL 32: 875; 1.8.15, PL 32: 877; 1.14.24, PL 32: 882. *De Trinitate* 12.15.24, CCL 50: 378. For Augustine's doctrine of illumination, see R. Jolivet, *Dieu soleil des esprits*, V. Bourke, *Augustine's Quest of Wisdom*, pp. 112-117, 216-217, 232-233. E. Gilson, *The Christian Philosophy of Saint Augustine*, pp. 77-111.

[29] See E. Gilson, "Pourquoi saint Thomas a critiqué saint Augustin," *Archives d'histoire doctrinale et littéraire du moyen âge* 1 (1926), 5-127.

[30] William of Auvergne, *De anima* 7. 6; *Opera omnia* 2: 211. According to William we need a special illumination (*illuxio*) in order to know God in this life.

[31] See St. Bonaventure, *Quaestio disputata de scientia Christi*, ed. Quaracchi, 5: 17-27. See J. F. Quinn, *The Historical Constitution of St. Bonaventure's Philosophy*, p. 529.

regarded as sufficient for us to know whatever comes within its natural range.[32] He identified this light with the agent intellect—that power of the soul so enigmatically described by Aristotle.[33] It is not, as Avicenna thought, a separate substance outside the soul enlightening it with ideas.[34] Rather, it is a created power within the person whereby he participates in the uncreated and divine light of knowing.[35] Thus, according to Aquinas, "God is constantly at work in the mind, endowing it with its natural light and giving it direction."[36] Augustine and Thomas Aquinas both affirm, but with different interpretations, the scriptural assurance that when we know, we are bathed in the divine light: "The light of your countenance, O Lord, is signed upon us."[37] If the natural and created light of our mind were not adequate to know the truth, but needed a new illumination (so Thomas Aquinas argues), neither would the added light, being created, be sufficient, but it would need a new illumination. This process would go on to infinity, with the result that we would never know the truth. The first light, therefore, must be adequate to know the truth without any additional illumination.[38]

The issue at stake between Aquinas and the Augustinians was not whether God illumines the mind, but how he does it. For Thomas, the illumination takes place without derogating from the mind's natural efficacy. Etienne Gilson succinctly sums up the difference between the Thomist and Augustinian views of knowledge in the following words:

> In St. Thomas, man receives from God everything he receives from Him in St. Augustine, but not in the same way. In St. Augustine, God delegates his gifts in such a way that the very insufficiency of nature constrains it to return toward him; in St. Thomas, God delegates His gifts through the mediacy of a stable nature which contains in itself—divine subsistence

---

[32] See Q. 1, a. 1, below, p. 17. See *De veritate* 9.1, ad 18.
[33] Aristotle, *De anima* 3.6 (430a15-19).
[34] See Q. 1, a. 1, below, p. 16.
[35] St. Thomas, *Summa theol.* 1.84.5.
[36] See Q. 1, a. 1, Reply to 6, below p. 19.
[37] Psalm 4:7. See Q. 1, a. 1, below pp. 17, 19. For St. Augustine, see *Confessions* 9. 4 (10-11), CCL 27: 139.74-75.
[38] See Q. 1, a. 1, below p. 15.

being taken for granted—the sufficient reason of all its operations. Accordingly, it is the introducing into each philosophical problem of a *nature* endowed with sufficiency and efficacy that separates thomism from augustinism. This teaching troubled augustinians because it seemed to confer on creatures a dangerous sufficiency. It enabled one to define with rigorous precision the respective domains of the natural and supernatural, indeed of philosophy and theology.[39]

## E.  THE NECESSITY OF FAITH

While defending the innate capacity of the mind to exercise its proper function, which is to know the truth, Thomas was well aware of its limitations and imperfections. Its natural knowledge often falls short of certitude and reached only probability. This is the case with the natural and practical sciences, and also with metaphysics, which aims at a knowledge of God.[40] Though it is possible to know something about him by natural reason, the supernatural illumination of faith is necessary to assure mankind an easy and certain path to him.[41] Besides the light of faith God illumines the mind in other ways, elevating it to acts of knowing beyond its natural powers. Such, for example, is the gift of prophecy and the gifts of the Holy Spirit, especially knowledge and understanding, which render the soul docile to divine inspiration and flower in mystical experience. In the next life the intellect is strengthened by the light of glory so that it can see God face to face.[42]

The necessity of faith, both natural and supernatural, is the theme of Question Three, Article One. Thomas has little to say here about the nature of faith; he will probe this topic in depth in his *Summa theologiae*.[43] The main lines of his teaching, however, can already

---

[39] E. Gilson, summary of seminar given in the École des Hautes Études (1922), quoted in L. K. Shook, *Etienne Gilson*, p. 397.

[40] Q. 6, a. 1, ad sec. quaest., ed Decker, pp. 208-209, trans. Maurer, pp. 67-69.

[41] See Q. 3, a. 1, Reply to 3, below, p. 68.

[42] On prophecy see *Summa theol.* 2-2. 171; on the gifts of the Holy Spirit, ibid. 2-2.8; on the light of glory 1.12.2.

[43] Ibid. 2-2.1-7.

be discerned in this early work. He adopts the traditional placing of faith between opinion and science. It is like opinion because it concerns objects that are not evident or clear to the mind. It differs from it, however, in that it gives firm assent to its object. In this respect it resembles science or understanding. The person who says, "It is my opinion..." or "It seems to me..." inclines to a certain position but does not fully commit himself to it for fear that the opposite may be true. One who doubts, wavers between two contrary positions without taking a stand between them. The believer firmly commits himself and gives his definite assent to something, not because it is evident to him, but because he has good reason to take the word of someone else that it is true.[44]

Thomas appeals to experience to show the necessity of faith. On the purely human level we often have to take another's word for what we cannot see for ourselves, for example objects beyond our perception and the thoughts of other persons. Without faith society would be impossible, as Cicero pointed out long ago. Lying and deceiving are always wrong, for they offend against the trust we must have in our fellow men. In the sciences, too, there is need of faith. The beginner must take the word of his instructor until the day when he can see the truth for himself.[45] The sciences themselves are interdependent: one science frequently presupposes truths proved or clarified in another. Metaphysics comes last in the pedagogical order and it borrows from all the sciences for its enrichment. They in turn depend on metaphysics for the elucidation and defence of the absolutely first principles.[46]

Besides purely human faith there is need of a divine gift of faith motivating us to assent with certainty to the word of God revealed in Scripture. This is an inner light or grace calling forth a human response in an assent to the divine word. Thomas conceived this divine gift as a *habitus*, that is, a stable possession of the soul, enriching its life and rendering it capable of cognitive acts beyond its natural powers.[47] The light of our mind with which we are naturally

---

[44] See Q. 3, a. 1, below, p. 65.
[45] Ibid. p. 66. See *De veritate* 14. 10; *Summa theol.* 2-2.2.3.
[46] See Q. 3, a. 1, below, p. 66. See also Q. 5, a. 1, and ibid. Reply to 9, ed. Decker, p. 166.1-6, and pp. 172.3-173.4, trans. Maurer, pp. 14-15 and 23-24.
[47] See *Summa theol.*, 2-2.4.1.

endowed disposes us to assent to self evident first principles, like the principle of non-contradiction, and the truth of the principles themselves moves us to assent to conclusions drawn from them. Probabilities incline us to form opinions; if the probabilities grow in strength they give rise to the human faith spoken of above. The faith that comes to us as a gift of God belongs to a new and higher order: it moves us to assent to truths with more certainty than any human motive. Human powers may fail and be deceived, "but the light of faith, which is, as it were, a faint stamp of the First Truth in our mind, cannot fail, any more than God can be deceived or lie."[48]

Though infused faith is a light leading us to assent to a revealed truth, it does not act directly on the intellect but on the will, with the result that we do not see what we believe nor are we compelled to assent to it, but we give our assent lovingly and voluntarily. To the objection that we should not assent uncritically or without reason, especially to matters beyond the range of our natural powers, Thomas replies that the assent of faith is not contrary to reason, "for natural reason maintains that we should assent to the words of God."[49] We have reasons for believing in God's word (later called "motives of credibility"), but they are not sufficient to elicit the act of faith; for this, divine grace is needed.

Faith, then, comes to us from within as a divine illumination, but it also has an external source, for as St. Paul says, "faith comes from hearing."[50] The believer must hear the word of God—or read it in the Scriptures—to give assent to it. Objects are proposed for his belief through a revelation in the Scriptures. Thomas speaks of these object as "realities...proposed from without."[51] The same realistic attitude toward the objects of faith is found in his *Summa theologiae*, which describes them as the realities themselves in which we believe, the first of which is God.[52] Of course we formulate our beliefs in propositions, as he goes on to say, and thus in a sense

---

[48] See Q. 3, a. 1, Reply to 4, below, p. 69; *Summa theol.* 2-2. 4. 8.
[49] See Q. 3, a. 1, Reply to 5, below, p. 70.
[50] Ibid., Reply to 4. Paul, Romans 10:17.
[51] Ibid.
[52] *Summa theol.* 2-2.1.1.

these may be called the objects of belief, but he insists that belief does not have for its goal a proposition but a reality.[53]

Thomas' doctrine of divine faith is firmly grounded in Scripture and the writings of the Church Fathers, but it is hardly comprehensible to the modern secularist, the boundaries of whose world are drawn by sensible experience. But while faith remains a mystery, it is intelligible in the Christian world of Aquinas, in which all of our knowledge of the truth has its primal origin in a divine illumination. Faith is but one extraordinary and gratuitous way which God has devised to disclose his own knowledge to the world.

Thomas argues that faith is a vital necessity for us, for without it we lack a sure guide to human destiny, which is perfect happiness in the vision and love of God.[54] From childhood we need faith in order to learn about God and to orient our lives toward him. Though it is possible to know something about God through natural reason, and some persons actually do so, it was necessary for God to reveal even those truths about himself that come within the range of reason. Thomas gives five reasons for this, taking a leaf from the Jewish theologian Maimonides.[55] The first is the profundity and difficulty of the subject, which conceal God from the human mind. The second is the weakness of the mind, especially in one's early years. The third is the lack in many persons of the preliminary knowledge and mental cultivation, especially in the sciences, that are needed for human reason to reach a knowledge of God. If God had not revealed himself, a large part of the human race would have been left without a knowledge of him. The fourth is physical incapacity, which prevents many from developing their mental powers to the point of knowing God. The fifth is a busy life, leaving little leisure to acquire the necessary knowledge about God.[56]

For these reasons it was necessary for God to provide us with faith in truths about himself that we could learn by ourselves but that few would otherwise actually come to know, and only with difficulty and many errors. Besides these naturally knowable truths

---

[53] Ibid. 1.2.c and ad 2.
[54] See J. Owens, *Human Destiny*, ch. 2.
[55] See Maimonides, *The Guide of the Perplexed*, I. 34.
[56] See Q. 3, a. 1, below, pp. 66-67.

about God there are others that are completely beyond human reason in the present life, such as his unity and trinity. These will be clearly seen in the next life, when our happiness will be complete. Through faith, however, we are given a kind of introduction to them, preparing us for their full revelation in the world to come.

## F. FAITH AND RELIGION

After treating of faith, St. Thomas turns to the relation of faith to religion (Q. 3, a. 2). He describes both faith and religion as virtues, but of different kinds. Faith, like hope and love, is a theological virtue because it has God for its object.[57] Religion is a moral virtue; more specifically it is a part of the cardinal virtue of justice.[58] Justice prompts us to give everyone his due; religion motivates us to give God his due by subjecting ourselves to him and showing him devotion. Religion is the service and worship of God; more than that, it is the binding of one's self to this service. Thomas cites Augustine for the doubtful origin of the word "religion" in *religare*, which means to bind back, or in *reeligere*, which means to choose again. Religion is the voluntary choosing God again after having lost him by neglect. This binding and choosing can take the form of vows, by which persons dedicate their whole life to God and are therefore called "religious."[59]

The primary acts of religion are spiritual, like the acts of the theological virtues and the gifts of the Holy Spirit. We are not, however, pure spirits; we also have bodies, and so our veneration and service of God should include bodily acts. Thus we serve him with our whole being. Bodily acts of religion have the added value of arousing ourselves and others to mental acts directed to God. Besides acts relating to God, religion includes care of our neighbor, especially looking after the poor and neglected.[60]

---

[57] These virtues are called theological because they have God for their object, they put us on the straight path to him, they are given to us by him alone, and they are taught by his revelation in Scripture. See *Summa theol.* 1-2.62.1.

[58] Ibid. 60.3; 2-2.81.5.

[59] See Q. 3, a. 2, below, p. 72.

[60] Ibid., *On the contrary* 2, below, p. 71.

The relations between faith and religion are complex. Religion has a different object from faith and consequently the two are formally distinct. Materially, however, the act of faith belongs to the virtue of religion, for by it we submit ourselves to God and venerate him. In fact, the acts of all the virtues come under religion insofar as they are done as a service to God and as something owing to him. Faith, however, is the cause and source of religion. We would not show devotion to God and subject ourselves to him unless we believed that he is the creator and governor of the world and the rewarder of our acts.[61]

In the article that follows (Q. 3, a. 3) St. Thomas takes up the theme of the catholicity or universality of the true faith. It is universal in its members because it is destined for all men and women. In fact, it has been accepted by persons in every state of life. Before the coming of Christianity different nations worshiped various gods. Only the Jewish people knew the true God. The prophets, under the inspiration of the Holy Spirit, foretold the coming of a universal religion, and this prophecy was fulfilled by the Catholic faith. This faith is also universal in its teachings. Unlike the pagan religions and philosophies, it is a way of life leading not only to eternal beatitude but also to temporal blessings. It instructs mankind in both spiritual and temporal matters. In short, it benefits the whole person, soul and body. It offers remedies for the liberation of the whole human race. The Catholic religion, moreover, has spread almost to the ends of the earth. For all these reasons the true faith merits the title "Catholic."[62]

## G. THE TRINITY

In Question Three, Article Four, Thomas comes to the main topic of Boethius' treatise: the Catholic doctrine of the Trinity. Boethius defended the orthodox belief that the Father, Son and Holy Spirit are not three gods but one God. He opposed the heresy of the Arians, who, he said, broke up the divine unity and parceled it out in unequal

---

[61] Ibid., below, p. 74.

[62] Ibid., below, p. 76; Reply to 2, p. 77; St. Thomas' Literal Commentary, below, pp. 58-59.

degrees of perfection in the three persons. It was inevitable, then, that they should posit a difference (*differentia*) or diversity (*diversitas*) between the persons, whereas the true belief denies any difference or otherness (*alteritas*) in the Trinity and affirms the unity of the three persons.[63]

Thomas traces the heresy of Arius to the Platonists, and more especially to Origen, whose conception of the Trinity was influenced by the Neoplatonic triad of the One, the *Nous* (or Intelligence), and the World Soul.[64] Plotinus taught that the *Nous* is a subordinate emanation from the One and the World Soul in turn an emanation from the *Nous*.[65] Origen (who was a fellow student with Plotinus under Ammonius Saccas in Alexandria) conceived the Son and Holy Spirit as less in dignity that the Father and indeed as his creatures.[66]

In his literal commentary on the text of Boethius preceding Question Three, Article Four, Aquinas stays close to the language and reasoning of the Roman theologian. He points out that Boethius is intent on denying any difference or otherness in the three persons and therefore any degrees of perfection among them. In order to substantiate this, Boethius describes three ways in which things can be different. They may differ in species, like a man and an ox; or in genus, like a man and a stone; or in number, like two men. Things are different in species by belonging to another species; they differ in genus by belonging to another genus, they differ in number by having different accidental characteristics. But clearly none of these types of difference is found in God. The persons do not differ in species or genus, nor do they differ in number through different

[63] See Boethius, *De Trinitate* 1, below, p. 57. Boethius here uses the terms "difference," "diversity," and "otherness" as synonyms. Thomas sometimes follows his example, but in their technical usage he distinguishes between difference and diversity. See Q. 4, a. 1, note 8. For an excellent commentary on this passage of Boethius, see J. J. E. Gracia, *Introduction to the Problem of Individuation in the Early Middle Ages*, pp. 97-107.

[64] See Q. 3, a. 4, below, p. 80. See *Contra gentiles* 4.6. On the influence of Origen's Neoplatonism on Arius, see J. Pelikan, *The Christian Tradition. A History of the Development of Doctrine*, 1: 195-200; E. Gilson, *History of Christian Philosophy in the Middle Ages*, pp. 52-53.

[65] Plotinus, *Enneads* 5.2.1.

[66] See J. Pelikan, *The Christian Tradition*, p. 191; E. Gilson, *History of Christian Philosophy*, pp. 35-43.

accidental traits. Therefore Thomas concludes with Boethius that there is no difference or inequality in the three persons of the Trinity.[67]

The principle underlying the reasoning of Boethius is that "the source of plurality is otherness (*alteritas*); apart from otherness plurality is unintelligible." As his examples of otherness show, he equates it with difference. He argues that because there is no otherness, understood as difference, between the divine persons, they are one.[68]

In Question Four, Article One, St. Thomas accepts the Boethian analysis of otherness as far as it goes, but he makes a deeper study of the axiom "the source of plurality is otherness." He points out that Boethius' analysis only takes into account the otherness of things differing in genus, species and number, and these kinds of difference are found only in things that are composed. For example, things differing in species, like a man and an ox, are composed of a genus (animal) and a specific difference (rational or irrational). Things differing in genus are likewise composed of a genus and a difference. Things differing in number are composed of substance and accidents. Since, according to both Boethius and Aquinas, the logical distinction between genus and difference presupposes the real distinction between form and matter, it can be said that Boethius' view of the source of plurality is restricted to things that have a real composition.

Probing more deeply into the factors that give rise to plurality, Thomas brings to light the otherness of simple and primary things. He cites as an example the otherness of the specific differences rational and irrational. They do not differ by a difference, but simply by themselves. In the strict sense of the word they are *diverse*, not different. If they differed, they would differ by still another difference, and one would have to posit something by which that difference differs from the other differences, and the process would go on to infinity. The conclusion is inevitable, therefore, that they are diverse by themselves. One is simply not the other.[69]

---

[67] St. Thomas' Literal Commentary, below, p. 60.

[68] See Boethius, *De Trinitate* 1, below, p. 57. Boethius derived his analysis of difference from Porphyry's *Isagoge*, which he translated into Latin and commented on twice. See Boethius, *In Isagogen Porphyrii commenta*, editio prima, 2.1, CSEL 48: 85-98; editio secunda, 2.5, CSEL 48: 183-197.

[69] See Q. 4, a. 1, below, pp. 89-90.

Another example offered by Aquinas is the otherness between creatures and God. Each creature is divided from God and from every other creature by itself: it *is* itself and it *is not* God or another creature; and thus divided they constitute a plurality. Not being God is contained in the very being of the creature; it is not the result of some intermediary factor. Similarly the being of every creature contains not being another creature. It is the primal opposition of being and non-being, expressed by the affirmation "It is" and the negation "It is not," that is the basic reason and ground of the division and plurality of things.[70]

This eliminates, in Thomas' view, the need of Avicenna's explanation of plurality. The Persian philosopher held as an axiom that from one cause only one effect can immediately follow. From this he concluded that God can be the immediate cause of only one effect, the first celestial Intelligence. God and this Intelligence then constitute a plurality, and from them a plurality of creatures can emerge. But if Thomas' analysis of otherness is correct, there is no need to postulate an intermediary, such as the primal Intelligence of Avicenna, to account for the plurality of creatures. All creatures are immediately related to God as their first cause whom they imitate in various degrees. As Thomas says, "...there can be several first effects [of the First Cause], in each of which there is present the negation both of its cause and of the other effect...".[71]

In the conceptual order, Thomas sees the notion of plurality arising in the following way. Our first notions are "being" and "non-being."[72] From them we at once form the concept of unity, for "one" simply means undivided being. After the division of being and non-being we also immediately conceive the plurality of prior and simple things, like the specific differences "rational" and "irrational." There follows the notion of diversity, which means that one item, when compared with another, is seen not to be the other. Thus the notion of diversity is a consequence of the notion of plurality, and it retains the force of the primal opposition between being and non-being. After conceiving the plurality of primary and simple

---

[70] Ibid., p. 90.
[71] Ibid., p. 90.
[72] See St. Thomas, *De veritate* 1.1.

items, we move to the notion of the division and plurality of secondary and composite ones, for example, the specific notions of man and ox. But the plurality of composite things depends on the plurality and division of those that are simple and primary, and these in turn owe their diversity to the opposition of being and non-being. "In this way," Thomas concludes, "the diversity of primary items causes the plurality of secondary ones."[73]

Thomas does not apply his analysis of otherness to the Trinity, no doubt because he did not complete his commentary on the treatise of Boethius. Had he done so, he would have had occasion to draw important consequences regarding the Trinity from his deepened notion of otherness. We can surmise what some of them would have been, however, if we examine his trinitarian doctrine in his later writings.

One of the most significant consequences is a more profound notion of the oneness of God. In order to avoid the Arian heresy Boethius denied any *difference* in God, understood as otherness in species, genus and number (in the sense of a multitude of substances differing by their accidental characteristics). In this perspective the essence of God is one and undivided because it contains none of these differences. Thomas goes further and shows that God is one not only in the Boethian sense, but more basically in that there is no *diversity* in him, in the way that one thing simply *is not* another. The divine essence is one and undivided in the persons of the Trinity; the essence of the Father is not other than the essence of the Son or Holy Spirit.[74] If they were diverse, God would contain the primary opposition between being and non-being, for, as we have seen, this gives rise to diversity. But there can be no non-being in God; he is the fullness and purity of Being. Indeed, he is subsistent being itself: *ipsum esse per se subsistens*.[75] He is one, then, or undivided, because

---

[73] See Q. 4, a. 1, below, p. 91.

[74] In order to avoid the error of Arius, Thomas warns that the following expressions should be avoided when speaking of the persons of the Trinity: "diversity" and "difference," which deny the unity of the divine essence; "division" and "separation," which are opposed to the divine simplicity; "disparity," which is opposed to the equality of the persons; and "alien" and "discrepant," which deny the likeness of the persons. *Summa theol.* 1.31.2; *De potentia* 9. 8..

[75] *Summa theol.* 1.4.2.

his essence is one and absolutely simple. And because his essence is identical with his existence (*esse*) the same can be said of his existence.[76] In short, he is one being and therefore one God.

The radical oneness of God would seem to preclude the possibility of a trinity of persons, and indeed in the proper sense of the terms there is no difference or diversity between them. The terms "difference" and "diversity" in their strict usage have to do with forms or essences, and so they are not applicable to the persons of the Trinity, which have the same divine essence. Each person is really identical with the one divine essence, and thus it enjoys the fullness of divine being. Nevertheless, the persons are really *distinct* from each other. The Father is distinct from the Son and both are distinct from the Holy Spirit. Thomas finds the general term "distinction" most appropriate to express the otherness of the persons in the Trinity.[77] As for the nature of this distinction, he specifies that they are distinct not in the order of essence or being but in the order of relation. As Boethius says, following Augustine, "relation brings about the Trinity."[78] Thomas continues this theological notion of the persons of the Trinity, while enriching it with his own philosophical views. Each person, in his perspective, is a distinct relation which—unlike the Aristotelian category of relation—is a supposit or person. In short, the divine person is a subsistent relation. Boethius warned that the Aristotelian categories take on an entirely new meaning when applied to the Trinity, and this is certainly true of relation. The person of the Father is Fatherhood, opposed to the person of the Son, who is Sonship. As such, each can be called *other* in the personal sense (*alius*), but not different or diverse, for he is not different or diverse in essence or being.[79] Thomas on one occasion speaks of a divine person having another mode of existing (*alium modum existendi*), because he is another relation, distinct from the relations of the other persons.[80] In this way there arises within the deity—in the words

---

[76] The divine persons have one being (*esse*). *Summa theol.* 1.30.4, ad 3.

[77] *De potentia* 9.8, ad 2.

[78] Boethius, *De Trinitate* 6, edd. Stewart, Rand, and Tester, p. 28.8-9. See St. Augustine, *De Trinitate* 5.11-14, CCL 50: 218-223.

[79] *Summa theol.* 1.31.2.

[80] *De potentia* 2.1, ad 13.

of Thomas—"a transcendent multitude."[81] This gives us another
and unexpected verification of the Boethian principle that "otherness
is the source of plurality."


## H. INDIVIDUATION

We have already noted that Boethius accounts for the numerical
difference between individuals by the diversity of their accidental
characteristics. Three men, for example, are not different in genus
or species but in their accidental traits: one is white and the other
black, one is tall and the other short, and so on. Thus the men are
many in number owing to the difference of their accidents.[82]

In his literal commentary on the text of Boethius, Thomas remarks
that someone might object that an accident can be present or absent
without destroying its subject. Therefore accidents can be removed
from their subject—either actually when it is a question of separable
accidents like sitting or standing, or in thought when it is a question
of inseparable accidents like masculine or feminine—without elim-
inating the subject of the accidents. So it would seem that accidents
have nothing to do with the multiplication of individual substances
in a species.[83] He points out that Boethius meets this objection by
appealing to the accident of place. For even though all accidents
were removed from a substance—at least mentally—there is one
accidental difference that cannot be eliminated, namely difference
in place. Two bodies cannot occupy the same place in reality or in
our imagination.[84]

When Thomas debates at length whether numerical difference is
caused by accidents (Q. 4, a. 2), he pays scant attention to the
Boethian doctrine. As we shall see, he himself gives a central role
to the accident of quantity in explaining individuation, but as for the

---

[81] *Summa theol.* 1.30.3, ad 2.

[82] Boethius, *De Trinitate* 1, below, p. 57. For Boethius' doctrine of individuation,
see J. J. E. Gracia, *Introduction to the Problem of Individuation in the Early Middle
Ages*, pp. 65-121.

[83] St. Thomas' Literal Commentary, below, p. 62. For the distinction between
separable and inseparable accidents, see St. Thomas, *Quaestiones de anima* 12, ad 7.

[84] Boethius, *De Trinitate* 1, below, p. 57.

other kinds of accidents, they "are not," he says, "the principle of individuation, though they are the cause of our knowing the distinction between individuals."[85] In other words we recognize individuals by their accidental differences, but they are not the cause of individuation. As for the special role Boethius accords to place in this connection, Thomas holds that according to the laws of nature two bodies cannot occupy the same place at the same time, but by a miracle this is possible.[86] Difference of place, then, like the difference of other accidents, with the exception of quantity, is an indication rather than a cause of numerical diversity.

In ascribing to accidents the role of individuation, Boethius betrays the influence of Neoplatonism. Porphyry's *Isagoge*, which Boethius translated into Latin and twice commented on, describes an individual as a thing "composed of a collection of characteristics which can never be the same for another; for the characteristics of Socrates could not be the same for any other particular man."[87] In short, an individual is a unique bundle of properties or characteristics. Commenting on Porphyry, Boethius takes these properties to be accidents, like the baldness and snubnoseness of Socrates.[88] This agrees with his position in the *De Trinitate* that individuals in a species are different in number owing to the variety of their accidents. In this view, it is the bundle of accidental characteristics that individuates the substance. In his commentary on Aristotle's *Categories*, however, Boethius takes the seemingly different position that accidents depend on substance and hence are individuated by it. In this perspective, substances individuate accidents rather than the converse.[89]

---

[85] See Q. 4, a. 2 below, p. 98. Boethius did not always clearly distinguish between accidents as the principle of discernibility of individuals and as the principle or cause of individuation. See J. J. E. Gracia, *Introduction to the Problem of Individuation*, p. 110.

[86] See Q. 4, a. 3, Reply to 1, below, p. 106. Thomas likely refers to the miracle of Christ's risen body passing through unopened doors. See John 20:19.

[87] Porphyry, *Isagoge*, trans. E. W. Warren, p. 41.22-24. Boethius, *In Isagogen Porphyrii commenta*, ed. secunda, 3. 11, CSEL 48: 234.14-18. The doctrine goes back to Plotinus, *Enneads* 6.3.8. See A. C. Lloyd, "Neoplatonic Logic and Aristotelian Logic, I and II," *Phronesis* 1 (1955), 158-159.

[88] Boethius, ibid., CSEL 48: 235.12.

[89] Boethius, *In categorias Aristotelis libri quatuor*, PL 64: 171-172. See J.J.E. Gracia, *Introduction to the Problem of Individuation*, pp. 85-86.

Before taking up the question of the principles diversifying individuals in a species, Thomas accounts for the other two diversities mentioned by Boethius: diversity in genus and species. He points out that the causes of all three diversities are to be found in the substantial being of things, which includes matter, form and the composite of the two. Diversity in genus is based on diversity of matter; diversity of species is founded on diversity of form; while diversity in number is grounded partly on diversity of matter and partly on diversity of accidents, especially on quantity and its dimensions.[90]

Although the analysis that follows makes use of logical notions such as genus and species, it is not in Thomas' intention a logical but a metaphysical investigation. He is searching for the real principles or causes that bring about the real differences in things located in genera, species, or described as individuals. He is not concerned with genera and species as such, that is, with logical concepts, but with the diversity of things in genera and species.

In this realist perspective, Thomas explains that diversity in genus is taken from matter in two ways. First, through the diverse relations things can have to matter. Matter gives to a material substance its character as a subject: owing to its matter, it can receive form, and the composite of form and matter is then receptive of accidents. This affords a basis for the difference between the ten widest genera or categories described by Aristotle. Each of them is differently related to matter. Something in the genus of substance (for example, animal) is related to matter as one of its parts (the other part being substantial form). Something in the genus of quantity (for example, length) is related to matter as its measure. Quality in turn (for example, whiteness) is related to it as its disposition. Consequent upon these genera, things are located in the other seven genera. For example, as a result of a thing's possessing quantity it can be in the genus of place, and following upon its possessing the quality of whiteness it can be in the genus of relation, for it can be similar to other white things.

In a second way, diversity in genus is taken from matter from the fact that matter is perfected by form. By matter Thomas here means primary matter, or the pure potentiality to receive substantial form.

---

[90] See Q. 4, a. 2, below, p. 94.

It itself has no form, though it can receive form. It is at the opposite pole to the pure actuality which is God. By receiving form, matter shares to some degree in the divine actuality. Form is described by Thomas as "the likeness itself of the primary actuality [that is, God] existing in any matter."[91] Now some things share the divine likeness only to the extent that they subsist (for example, a stone), some to the extent that they live (for example, a plant), some to the extent that they have knowledge (for example, an animal), others to the extent that they understand (for example, a human being). These grades of perfection in things are the consequences of the reception in matter of more or less perfect substantial forms. Thomas hastens to add that any one substance has only one substantial form. He did not share the opinion of some of his contemporaries that there is a plurality of substantial forms in a substance giving it its various levels of substantial perfection. If this were true, he argued, the substance would not be *one*, for substantial form gives to a substance its substantial being and unity. The one substantial form gives to the substance all its substantial perfection. Thus the human soul, which is the substantial form of a human person, gives to him not only his capacity to understand but also all his lesser substantial perfections, such as existence, life and the capacity for sense perception.[92]

These remarks set the stage for Thomas' explanation of how difference in genus is based on matter in its relation to form. Several substances sharing unequally the divine actuality will always have something in common. For example, an animal and a plant are alike in being alive, and on the basis of this common factor we conceive the genus "living body." Thomas calls the common factor from which the genus is taken "matter" or "material," not in the sense of primary matter, which is devoid of all form, but in the sense that it is open to further generic determinations. Thus we can add to the genus "living body" the perfection "sentient" (that is, having the capacity to feel and perceive) and the imperfection "non-sentient."

---

[91] Ibid., p. 95. For the notions of matter and form, see E. Gilson, *The Christian Philosophy of St. Thomas Aquinas*, pp. 175-178.

[92] See E. Gilson, ibid. pp. 193-195. For the history of the problem of the plurality of forms, see idem, *History of Christian Philosophy in the Middle Ages*, pp. 416-420; J. F. Quinn, *The Historical Constitution of St. Bonaventure's Philosophy*, pp. 219-319.

This gives rise to the different genera of animal and plant. In this way, Thomas says, matter "is the principle of diversity in genus inasmuch as it underlies a common form."[93]

The various genera are in turn receptive of specific differences resulting in the variety of species. Thus the genus "animal" is differentiated into species by the addition of the specific differences "rational" and "irrational." Thomas conceives these differences as formal principles related to genera as form to matter. Form, then, can be said to be the principle of specific diversity, as, in the sense explained above, matter is the principle of generic diversity.

Neither form nor matter, however, when considered just in themselves or abstractly, can be the cause of the numerical diversity of individuals in the same species. A form as such is predicable of many individuals, as man is predicable of many human beings. This is contrary to an individual, which is not predicable of many subjects. The human form, however, can be rendered individual by being received in matter—not in matter in general, but in particular matter, determined to *this* place and to *this* time. The determination of matter comes about by the accident of quantity with its three dimensions, for dimensive quantity allows matter to be divided into parts, each of which can receive the same form, though diversified in number. Thus the principle of individuation, or the cause of numerical diversity, is matter as subject to quantity and its dimensions.[94]

This explanation of individuation should not be taken as a process things undergo as they gradually become more and more particular, beginning with the most universal status as genera and ending as individuals. For Aquinas, only individuals exist and are real. His analysis determines the factors in the metaphysical structure of the individual that make possible a differentiation of species in a genus and a numerical diversity of individuals in a species. In accounting for the latter possibility, the accident of quantity with its three dimensions is shown to play a crucial role.

We usually think of dimensions as definite measurements in length, depth, width, etc. Understood in this way, Thomas here contends,

---

[93] See Q. 4, a. 2, below, p. 98. See St. Thomas, *De ente et essentia* 2, ed. Leonine 43: 372.169-183. *In V. Meta.* lect. 22, n. 1123.

[94] See Q. 4, a. 2, ibid.

dimensions cannot be the principle of individuation, because the same individual often varies in its exact dimensions. If they were the cause of individuation, with a change of dimensions the individual would cease to be numerically the same. As a person grew taller, he would not be the same individual he was before. In order to avoid this difficulty, Thomas appeals to indeterminate dimensions as the cause of individuation. By this he means the *nature* of dimensions, without their exact delimitation. Of course, when dimensions *exist* they are always definite, but of themselves they have a nature—though an incomplete one—in the genus of quantity. Through these indeterminate dimensions, matter is rendered *this* designated matter (*haec materia signata*) and individuates form.[95]

Thomas resorts here, and also in his commentary on the *Sentences*,[96] to Averroes' notion of undetermined dimensions to account for the individuation of material substances. Some historians contend that he abandoned this account of individuation in favor of individuation by matter with determined dimensions.[97] They point out that later on in his commentary on the *De Trinitate* he maintains that matter is the principle of individuation as it exists with determined dimensions.[98] In the contemporary *On Being and Essence* he asserts that the principle of individuation is *materia signata*, which he describes as matter considered as the subject of determined dimensions.[99] Others deny any change in Thomas' doctrine, arguing that there is only an apparent discrepancy in the two accounts of individuation.[100] It is

---

[95] Ibid.

[96] *Sent.* 2,d.3, q.1, a.4; ed. Mandonnet, 2: 97: "It is impossible to understand different parts in matter unless you understand beforehand in matter dimensive quantity, at least undefined, through which it is divided, as the Commentator (Averroes) says in his *De substantia orbis*, 1, and in 1 *Physics.*" For Averroes' doctrine of individuation, see M.-D. Roland-Gosselin, *Le «De ente et essentia» de s. Thomas d'Aquin*. pp. 67-70; L. Elders, *Faith and Science*, p. 72.

[97] See M.-D. Roland-Gosselin, *Le «De ente et essentia»*, p. 109; I. Klinger, *Das Prinzip der Individuation bei Thomas von Aquin*.

[98] See Q. 5, a. 2 and Reply to 1, ed. Decker, p. 176.19-20 and 177.14-15, trans. Maurer, pp. 28, 29.

[99] *De ente et essentia* 2, ed. Leonine 43: 371.73-77.

[100] See U. Degli'Innocenti. "Il pensiero di san Tommaso sul principio d'individuazione," *Divus Thomas* (Piacenza) 45 (1942) 35-81. J. Bobik. "La doctrine de s. Thomas sur l'individuation des substances corporelles," *Revue philosophique de Louvain* 51 (1953), 5-41; "Dimensions in the Individuation of Bodily Substances,"

beyond the scope of this Introduction to attempt to settle the dispute. It can be said with certainty, however, that Thomas' consistent position is that matter with the dimensions that determine it are the twofold principle of the individuation of material substances.[101]

The problem that led Thomas to adopt the Averroist notion of undetermined dimensions: how can an individual remain identical with a change of dimensions? vanishes if we take into account the other factors contributing to individuality. Matter plays a passive role in individuation, making possible the multiplication of form in many individuals. But matter with its dimensions exists only through form, and both form and matter exist only through the act of existing (*esse*) that posits an individual substance in the real world. Once in possession of its own form and *esse*, the individual remains identical in number despite accidental changes, such as differences in dimension. In the last analysis, it is owing to its act of existing (*esse*), which is never common but proper to the individual, that a being is a numerically distinct individual.[102]

## I. CONCLUSION

The distance between Boethius' *De Trinitate* and Thomas Aquinas' commentary on it is obvious. Aquinas' little treatise belongs to a different intellectual world from that of Boethius. They are separated by seven hundred years of time, but more importantly by a new mentality which originated in the complex of intellectual forces of the thirteenth century, the chief of which was the discovery of the works of Aristotle and his Muslim commentators. Boethius and Thomas shared the same faith, but each reflected on it in the framework of

---

*Philosophical Studies* 4 (1954) 60-79. L. Elders sees only a verbal difference between Thomas' various accounts of individuation. See his *Faith and Science*, pp. 66-81. See also J. Owens' forthcoming article, "Thomas Aquinas: Dimensive Quantity as Individuating Principle," *Mediaeval Studies* 50 (1988).

[101] See *Contra gentiles* 4.65; *Summa theol.* 3.77.2; *Quodlibet* 11.6.6, ad 2.

[102] Thus Thomas writes: "A substance is individuated through itself, whereas accidents are individuated through their subject, which is a substance; for we speak of this whiteness inasmuch as it is in this subject." *Summa theol.* 1.29.1 c. See E. Gilson, *The Christian Philosophy of St. Thomas Aquinas*, p. 372 and p. 470, n. 10; D. Winiewicz, "A Note on *alteritas* and Numerical Diversity in St. Thomas Aquinas," *Dialogue* 16 (1977), 693-707.

his own time and culture. Thomas did not deny anything Boethius said. Rather, he nourished his thought upon it, as he did upon the vast literature of the Church Fathers and his medieval predecessors, embracing all that he found valid in them in his own theology. The result was a new development and enrichment of Christian doctrine. In substance it remained the same "discourse" about God and the mysteries of salvation that it was in the age of Augustine and Boethius, but it was now renovated and deepened by fresh insights that were possible only in the medieval world.

Essential elements in the Thomistic renewal of theology were the literary, scientific and philosophical achievements of his age. Theology lives and thrives on these resources, using them in its effort to understand more adequately the revealed word of God. Thomas shared these resources with his fellow theologians, and he brought to them a rare philosophical acumen and depth of insight. Ever busy raising new questions and offering novel solutions, as his friend and biographer William of Tocco relates, he brought theology and philosophy to their peak in the thirteenth century. [103]

The span of seven hundred years that separates us from Aquinas is the same as that which removed him from the Roman world of Boethius. Modern theologians and Christian philosophers live in a new mental climate which presents them at once with new resources and unforeseen problems. Vatican II pointed out that "recent studies and findings of science, history, and philosophy raise new questions which influence life and demand new theological investigations." [104] Commenting on theology's task after Vatican II, Yves Congar points out that modern philosophy's reflection on man's situation and existential experience offer new resources to theology. He continues: "We cannot, a priori, exclude the philosophy of existence and of the personal subject, or the anthropological sciences, or the biblical criticism and the string of its corollaries." [105] Though Aquinas knew none of this, today it can all be included in the ratio which, he claims, theology should bring to bear upon the mysteries of faith. But the theologian should also, following Thomas' injunction, oppose

[103] Acta sanctorum 7: 661, c.3, n.15.
[104] The Documents of Vatican II, ch. 2, ed. W. M. Abbott, p. 268, n. 62.
[105] Yves Congar, "Theology's Tasks after Vatican II," Theology of Renewal, ed. L. K. Shook, 1: 53.

whatever the world offers that is inimical to the faith. To quote Congar again:

> Our task is to be at once open-minded, receptive, and critical, that is, to exercise the critical function inherent in faith. This is an attitude very different from ignorance or disdain. It is an aspect of that contestation which faith, itself contested by the world, has to exercise in regard to the world. It is permissible to think that, not infrequently Christians have failed in their duty to contest the society in which they lived, and which was, and more than ever is today, contrary to the Gospel, to contest the doings of potentates, and also to contest the forms of their own doings and their own organizations. Yet this is a prophetic function of faith. [106]

As a living discipline, theology has the task of constantly strengthening and rejuvenating itself by scrutinizing its sources in Scripture, which contains the word of God, [107] by going to school with the Fathers and the great Scholastics, like Thomas and Bonaventure, by learning from the liturgy and the other monuments of our tradition, and by accepting the new resources of the modern world. [108] It is in this spirit that we offer the present translation of Thomas Aquinas' commentary on the *De Trinitate* of Boethius, Questions 1-4.

The translation was made from Bruno Decker's edition of the commentary, first published in 1955 and slightly revised in the reprint of 1959. I wish to thank the publisher, E. J. Brill, for permission to use this edition.

I have adopted Decker's corrections to his edition listed in his article "Corrigenda et Addenda à l'édition du 'In Boethium de Trinitate' de s. Thomas d'Aquin," *Scriptorium* 13 (1959), 81-82. C. Vansteenkiste had suggested improvements in the edition of 1955 in "Un

---

[106] Ibid.

[107] See *The Documents of Vatican* II, ch. 5, p. 127, n. 24.

[108] See Yves Congar, "Theology's Taskes after Vatican II," p. 65. See also Pope John Paul II, "Method and Doctrine of St. Thomas in Dialogue with Modern Culture," *Two Lectures on St. Thomas Aquinas.*

testo di San Tommaso in edizione critica," *Angelicum* 33 (1956), 437-442, as did P.-M. Gils in his review in *Scriptorium* 10 (1956), 111-120. Later, Gils published helpful notes on the 1959 reprint in *Bulletin thomiste* 11 (1960-1961), 41-44, n. 54.

Scriptural quotations have been taken from the *Revised Standard Version*, except in a few cases where the Douai version expresses more exactly the interpretation of Thomas Aquinas.

I am grateful to Walter H. Principe for his careful reading of the translation and for his many improvements and corrections. However, the responsibility for the translation is mine.

The place and date of publication of works cited in the Notes are given in the bibliography.

Armand Maurer
Pontifical Institute
of Mediaeval Studies

Thomas Aquinas

Commentary on the
*De Trinitate*
of Boethius,
Questions I-IV

# ST. THOMAS' INTRODUCTION

*I will seek her out from the beginning of her birth,*
*and will bring the knowledge of her to light* (Wisdom 6:24).


The natural gaze of the human mind, burdened by the weight of a perishable body,[1] cannot fix itself in the first light of truth, by which everything can be easily known. As a consequence, human reason in the development of its natural knowledge must advance from things that are posterior to those that are prior, and from creatures to God. As Romans 1:20 says: "Ever since the creation of the world his invisible nature, namely his eternal power and deity, has been clearly perceived in the things that have been made"; and Wisdom 13:5: "For from the greatness and beauty of created things comes a corresponding perception of their Creator." And this is what is said in Job 36:25: "All men see him," that is, God, "everyone beholds him from afar." For creatures, which are our natural means of knowing God, are infinitely distant from him. But because our power of sight is easily deceived about objects seen at a distance, those who try to know God from creatures have fallen into many errors. Thus it is said in Wisdom 14:11: "The creatures of God are...a snare to the feet of the unwise," and in Psalm 63:7: "They have failed in their search." Accordingly God has provided for the human race another, safe way of knowing, imparting his knowledge to the minds of men through faith, as is said in 1 Corinthians 2:11: "The things also that are of God no one knows, but the Spirit of God: but to us God has revealed them by his Spirit." This is the Spirit which makes us believers, as is said in 2 Corinthians 4:13: "Since we have the same spirit of faith... we too believe, and so we speak." Consequently, just as our natural knowledge begins with the knowledge of creatures obtained by the senses, so the knowledge imparted from above begins with the cognition of the first Truth bestowed on us by faith. As a

[1] See Wisdom 9:15: "...for a perishable body weighs down the soul, and this earthly tent burdens the thoughtful mind."

result the order of procedure is different in the two cases. Philosophers, who follow the order of natural knowledge, place the science of creatures before the science of God, that is to say, natural philosophy before metaphysics, but theologians follow the opposite path, placing the consideration of the creator before that of creatures.[2]

The latter order is the one followed by Boethius. Setting out to treat of matters of faith, he took as the starting point of his study the supreme source of things, namely the Trinity of the one God, free from all composition. So the words quoted above can be applied to him: "I will seek her out from the beginning of her birth, and bring the knowledge of her to light." In these words, insofar as they are relevant to the present short treatise (which Boethius addressed to Symmachus, a Roman patrician), we can observe three things: the subject matter of the treatise, its method, and its purpose.

The subject matter of the treatise is the Trinity of persons in the one divine essence. The Trinity originates in the primal birth by which the divine wisdom is eternally begotten by the Father, as we read in Proverbs 8:24: "The depths were not as yet, and I was already conceived," and in Psalm 2:7: "Today I have begotten you." This birth is the beginning of every begetting of another, for it alone perfectly takes on the nature of the begetter. All other births are imperfect, for in them the offspring receives a part of the begetter's substance or a likeness of it. Every other birth, then, must have its origin in a certain imitation of the primal birth, as Ephesians 3:15 says: "For this reason I bow my knees to the Father of our Lord Jesus Christ after whom all paternity in heaven and earth is named." Because of this, Colossians 1:15 calls the Son "the firstborn of every creature," pointing out the origin and likeness of giving birth, but not the same nature of begetting. So it is aptly said; "from the beginning of her birth"; and Proverbs 8:22 states: "The Lord possessed me in the beginning of his ways." Nor is the above-mentioned birth the beginning of creatures alone, but also of the Holy Spirit, who proceeds from the Begetter and his Offspring. From the fact, moreover, that Boethius does not say "I will seek out the beginning of her birth," but rather "I will seek her out from the beginning," he

---

[2] See St. Thomas, *Contra gentiles* 2.4.

indicates that his inquiry will not come to an end with this initial birth, but, starting with it, it will go on to other topics. In fact, Boethius' doctrine is divided into three parts. The first concerns the Trinity of persons, from whose procession every other birth or procession originates. In the present book[3] he treats of what we should know of the divine trinity and unity. In another, written for John, a deacon of the Roman church, and whose opening words are "I ask whether the Father," he discusses the mode of predication used regarding the Trinity of persons.[4] The second part, which concerns the procession of good creatures from the good God, is contained in the book addressed to the same John and entitled *De hebdomadibus*. Its opening words are "You ask me."[5] The third part has to do with the restoration of creatures by Christ. This is divided into two parts. First he sets forth the faith taught by Christ by which we are justified. This is contained in a book entitled *On Christian Faith*, which begins "The Christian faith."[6] Second, he explains what we should believe about Christ, how in him two natures come together in one person. This is found in the book *On Two Natures in the One Person of Christ*, written for the same John and beginning with the words "You indeed solicitously."[7]

The method used in treating of the Trinity is twofold, as Augustine says[8]: authority and reason.[9] Augustine combined both of these methods, as he himself states.[10] Some of the holy Fathers, like Ambrose[11]

---

[3] That is, Boethius' *De Trinitate*. The full title is: *Quomodo Trinitas unus Deus ac non tres dii* (How the Trinity is One God, not Three Gods), edd. Stewart, Rand and Tester, pp. 3-31.

[4] *Utrum Pater et Filius et Spiritus Sanctus de divinitate substantialiter praedicentur* (Whether Father, Son, and Holy Spirit are Substantially Predicated of the Divinity), ibid., pp. 33-37.

[5] Its full title is: *Quomodo substantiae in eo quod sint bonae sint cum non sint substantialia bona* (How Substances are Good in Virtue of their Existence without being Substantial Goods), ibid., pp. 38-51.

[6] *De fide catholica* (*On the Catholic Faith*), ibid., pp. 52-71. On the authenticity of this tractate, see John Mair, "The Text of the *Opuscula Sacra*," *Boethius. His Life, Thought and Influence*, ed. M. Gibson, pp. 206-207.

[7] *Liber contra Eutychen et Nestorium* (A Treatise against Eutyches and Nestorius), edd. Stewart, Rand, and Tester, pp. 73-129.

[8] St. Augustine, *De Trinitate* 1.2.4 and 1.2.3, CCL 50: 31-32 and 30-31.

[9] See St. Thomas, *Quodlibet* 4, q. 9, a. 3; *Contra gentiles* 1.2, 8, 9.

[10] St. Augustine, *De Trinitate* 1.2.3-4, CCL 50:30-32.

[11] St. Ambrose, *De fide*, PL 16: 527-698; *De Spiritu Sancto*, PL 16: 703-816.

and Hilary,[12] made use of only one of them, namely authority. Boethius, however, chose to pursue the other method, that of reasoning, taking for granted what the others had investigated by authority. The method adopted in the present treatise is suggested by the words "I will seek out," indicating a rational inquiry. This is in harmony with Ecclesiasticus 39:1: "The wise man will seek out", that is, he will investigate by reason, "the wisdom," that is, the knowledge of the Trinity, "of all the ancients," that is, which men of former times asserted on authority alone. So he begins the Preface with the words, "The problem that has been for so long the subject of our investigation."

The aim of the treatise is to clarify the mysteries of faith, as far as this is possible in the present life, following Ecclesiasticus 24:31, which says: "They who explain me shall have life everlasting." So Boethius adds: "and bring the knowledge of her to light," as we read in Job 28:11: "He has searched the depths of rivers, and hidden things he has brought forth to light."

---

[12] St. Hilary of Poitiers, *De Trinitate*, CCL 62.

# BOETHIUS' PREFACE
## ADDRESSED TO SYMMACHUS, HIS FATHER-IN-LAW [1]

The problem that has been for so long the subject of our investigation—to the extent that the divine light has deigned to enkindle the spark of my mind—now, having settled it by reasoning and having cast it in literary form, I venture to present to you and to share with you, being as eager for your judgment as I am devoted to the results of my work. What I have in mind in this regard, whenever I commend my thoughts to writing, you can glean both from the difficulty itself of the topic and also from the fact that I discuss it with the few—I may say with you alone. For I am not prompted to write by the vain desire of fame and empty popular applause, but if there be any external reward, it can only be the hope of a judgment in keeping with the topic. For, apart from yourself, wherever I have turned my eyes, they have encountered on the one hand laziness and indolence, and on the other hand jealousy and shrewdness, so that a man who casts these matters before such monsters to be trampled under foot rather than to be appreciated, would seem to bring discredit on the study of the things of God.

Therefore I write in a concise style, and the ideas I have taken from the most profound philosophical disciplines I envelop with meaningful new words, so that they may speak only to me and to you, if you ever turn your attention to them. The rest I disregard, so that those who cannot understand might be shown to be unworthy even to read them. But you ought to ask of me only as much as the insight of the human mind is capable of in mounting to the heights of the Godhead. Indeed, in other arts the same limit, so to speak, is set to which human reason may go. Medicine, for example, does not always restore the sick to health, but the doctor will not be blamed if he has omitted nothing that he ought to have done. The same is true with the other arts. In the present case the problem is

---

[1] Boethius, *De Trinitate*, edd. Stewart, Rand and Tester, pp. 2-5.

so difficult that it should be easier for the reader to be indulgent. You should also consider whether the seminal notions coming to me from the writings of St. Augustine have borne fruit in my work. And now let us turn to the proposed question.

## St. Thomas' Literal Commentary

The author introduces the treatise with a preface in which he makes three points. First, he briefly indicates the causes of the work, thus preparing his hearer to accept his teaching. Second, at the words, "Therefore I write in a concise style," etc., he adds an apology, thereby gaining his hearer's good will. Third, when he says, "You should also consider," etc., he points out that the inspiration of the work and its topic, so to speak, is the teaching of Augustine, in so doing catching his hearer's attention.

In the first part he explains the four causes of his book. First the material cause, when he says, "The problem that has been for so long the subject of our investigation," etc., namely the Trinity of persons of the one God. These words hint both at the difficulty of the subject, which demanded a lengthy inquiry, and also at the careful research he devoted "for so long" to the investigation. This is the sense in which "our investigation" may be understood, though it can also be taken to mean the inquiry undertaken by many persons, because from the beginning of the Church's existence this problem has vexed the brightest Christian minds.

Second, he indicates the efficient cause of the work: the proximate or secondary cause with the words "the spark of my mind," and the primary or principal cause with the phrase "the divine light has deigned to enkindle." The proximate cause of the inquiry was indeed the author's mind, which is correctly called a spark. Fire, as Dionysius says,[1] is best suited to express the divine properties, at once because of its subtlety, its light, its active force through heat, and its position and movement. These are especially fitting to God, who has the greatest freedom from composition and materiality, absolute clarity, almighty power, and the highest majesty. It applies to the angels

---

[1] Dionysius, *De caelestia hierarchia* 15.2, PG 3: 329A.

only in an inferior way, and to human minds in the lowest of all; for, owing to their union with the body, their purity is sullied, their light darkened, their power weakened, and their upward movement impeded. So the effectiveness of the human mind is aptly likened to a spark. Indeed, it is inadequate to investigate the truth of the present topic unless it were illumined by the divine light. The divine light is accordingly the principal cause, whereas the human mind is the secondary cause.

Third, he indicates the formal cause when he says "settled it by reasoning," and he suggests three points in his mode of procedure. First, the fact that he used the method of argumentation; thus he says "settled it by reasoning." For as long as a question is dubious and is debated pro and con with probable arguments, it remains as it were unsettled, and the truth is not yet certain. It is said to be settled when reason is brought to bear upon it, conferring on it the certainty of truth. In this he showed concern for understanding, because, as Augustine says,[2] what we believe we owe to authority, but what we understand we owe to reason. Second, the fact that he not only gave an oral lecture but also committed his words to writing; as he says, he "cast it in literary form." By so doing he showed concern for our memory. Third, the fact that he has written not as teaching those present, but in the style of a letter addressed to persons at a distance. Aristotle also composed his works in different styles. Some he wrote for an audience listening to him in his presence, and these books are called lectures, for example, the *Lectures on Physics*. Others he composed for those not present, for example, the treatise *On the Soul*, as is suggested in the *Ethics*,[3] where mention is made of "discourses for those at a distance," as the Greek commentator says.[4]

There follow the words, "I venture to present [my work] to you" as to one more expert for judgment, and "to share [it] with you" as with a companion for improvement. With these words he asks for

---

[2] St. Augustine, *De utilitate credendi* 11.25, CSEL 25 (pt. 1), 32-33.

[3] Aristotle, *Nic. Ethics* 1.13 (1102a26).

[4] Eustratius, *In Ethicam Nicomacheam. The Greek Commentaries on the Nicomachean Ethics of Aristotle in the Latin Translation of Robert Grosseteste* 1: 179.13, ed. H. P. F. Merchen. See St. Thomas, *In Eth.* 1, lect. 19, ed. Leonine 47: 68.94-69.101.

the hearer's opinion, and so he continues: "being as eager for your judgment as I am devoted to the results of my work." Because he was eager to reach the truth, he resolved the question at hand with rational arguments; because he was anxious for the opinion of Symmachus, he sent it to him in this reasoned form.

Fourth, he indicates the final cause when he says, "What I have in mind in this regard," that is, what my purpose is in the project just mentioned, "whenever I commend my thought to writing" about the question at hand or anything else, "you can glean both from the difficulty itself of the topic, and also from the fact that I discuss it," not with the rank and file, but "with the few," namely with learned men, "I may say with you alone." For he did not write the book to be read to the public, which is sometimes done to win the applause of the crowd, but only for one learned man. So he continues: "For I am not prompted," that is, to take up my pen, "by the vain desire," that is, the praise "of fame and empty popular applause," like the poets declaiming their verses in the theaters, because such popular acclaim is often mindless. Thus he eschews an unsuitable purpose and adopts a fitting one, suggesting that his main purpose is interior, namely the perception of divine truth, and explaining his secondary purpose, which is receiving the opinion of someone who is wise. So he continues: "but if there be any external reward," as though to say: I am urged on mainly by an inner satisfaction, but if there be an external reward, "it can only be the hope of a judgment in keeping with," that is, suited to, "the topic." As though to say: the only judgment I ask for as an external reward is one worthy of such a lofty subject. In this matter judgment ought not to be granted lazily to dullards or shrewdly to the envious, but only to a kindly learned man. Thus he continues: "For, apart from yourself, wherever I have turned my eyes," that is, wherever I have looked, except to you, "they have encountered on the one hand," that is, in some quarters, "laziness," that is stupidity, "and indolence," that is, slothfulness, "and on the other hand jealousy," that is, envy, "and shrewdness," that is, cleverness in doing harm, "so that a man who casts," that is, expounds in a disorderly fashion, "these matters," that is, divine realities, "before such monsters" (Men are called monsters who bear within their human bodies the heart of a beast; owing to sin they have become like beasts in their affections), "would seem to bring discredit on the study of the things of God." Thus these matters would be trampled under foot rather than approved by them, because they seek not so much to understand as—owing to their jealousy—to revile whatever is said. Thus it is said in Matthew 7:6: "Give not that which is holy to dogs." etc.[5]

"Therefore I write in a concise style," etc. This is the second part of the preface, in which he appends an apology. First, he apologizes for the difficulty of the work, second for its imperfection, beginning with the words, "But you ought to ask of me," etc. He mentions three difficulties which he readily ascribes to the treatise. The first arises from the brevity of his writing. Thus he says: "Therefore I write in a concise style." As Horace says, "I try to be brief, but I become obscure."[6] The second difficulty is a consequence of the subtle reasoning he introduces. This is what he means when he speaks of "ideas I have taken from the most profound philosophical disciplines. These are disciplines that abstract from sensible things and whose principles and conclusions he uses, for example, those of metaphysics and logic. The third obstacle results from the novelty of his language. Thus he says: "the ideas I have taken... I envelop with meaningful new words." They are called new either with reference to the present topic, because others who have treated of the question did not use the same language, or with reference to the readers who are unaccustomed to it. These three impediments he adds to a fourth which he mentioned before, namely the difficulty of the topic. Accordingly, what is written in the book is addressed only to the learned who could understand it, like the author himself and the person for whom the book is written. The rest, who are unable to comprehend it, are debarred from reading it. Indeed, it is not easy to read what is not understood. He begins this part with the word "therefore," which is the sign of a conclusion, because his reflections follow from what has gone before. But the text is clear.

Then when he says, "But you ought to ask of me," etc., he apologizes for a shortcoming in the work. In it one should not demand of him greater certainty than human reason is capable of in mounting

---

[5] Thomas adds as a sort of footnote a variant reading of Boethius' text: "Another version: Lest I too, if I did otherwise, 'might seem' (to bring discredit on the study of the things of God), 'who cast' (these matters before such monsters...)."

[6] Horace, *De arte poetica* 25.

to the heights of the Godhead. He proves this by an "argument from a lesser case" in the other arts, in which the goal of every master of the art is to accomplish as much as human reason allows. Thus a doctor does not always effect a cure, but if he neglects nothing that he ought to do, he will not be held at fault, and the same is true in the other arts. So also in the present work, which concerns a most difficult topic surpassing the powers of the human mind, the author ought to be shown greater indulgence if he does not solve the question with absolute certainty. Then, at the words "You should also," he points out whose authority he is following in his book, namely that of Augustine. Not that he simply repeats what is contained in Augustine's book, but that Augustine's statements about the Trinity—namely that the divine persons are the same with respect to what is absolute but distinct with respect to what is relative—he takes as seeds and principles and uses them to elucidate the difficulty of the question. Thus the unfolding of the truth through copious reasoning is a fruit springing forth in him from seeds sown by Augustine. But which may be fitting and fruitful he leaves to the judgment of the person for whom he is writing, as he takes up the question at hand.

# QUESTION ONE

# ON THE KNOWLEDGE OF DIVINE REALITIES[1]

Two questions arise here. The first concerns the knowledge of divine realities, the second has to do with making them known.
There are four questions regarding the first point:

1. Does the human mind need a new illumination by the divine light in order to know the truth?
2. Can the human mind arrive at a knowledge of God?
3. Is God what the mind first knows?
4. Is the human mind by itself able to arrive at a knowledge of the divine Trinity?

### ARTICLE ONE

*Does the Human Mind Need a New Illumination by the Divine Light in Order to Know the Truth?*[2]

*We proceed to the first article as follows:*

It seems that the human mind does need a new illumination by the divine light for the knowledge of any truth.

*1.* 2 Cor. 3:5 says: "Not that we are sufficient to think anything of ourselves, as of ourselves; but our sufficiency is from God." But

---

[1] Thomas frequently uses the notion of divine things or realities (*divina*). It primarily refers to God, who is divine by his nature, but the term is extended by analogy to anything related to him as its principle and end. See *Sent.* 1, d.2, divisio textus, ed. Mandonnet 1:59. The term can also be applied to anything great and wonderful. See St. Thomas, *Responsio ad magistrum Ioannem de Vercellis de 43 articulis*, n. 34, ed. Leonine 42:333. Thomas also calls divine whatever abstracts in existence from matter and motion; in short, the objects of metaphysics. See his Literal Commentary on Chapter Two, ed. Decker, p. 160.10-11, trans. Maurer, p. 7.

[2] See St. Thomas, *Summa theol.* 1.79.4, 1-2.109.1; *Sent.* 2, d. 17, q. 2, a. 1, and 2, d. 28, q. 1, a. 5; *Quodlibet* 10, q.4, a.1. On Thomas' doctrine of the mind's

there can be no perception of the truth without thought. Therefore the human mind cannot know a truth unless it is newly enlightened by God.

2.    It is easier to learn a truth from someone else than to see it by oneself. Thus, as is said in the *Ethics*,[3] those who know by themselves take precedence over those who can learn from others. But no one can learn from others unless God teaches his mind from within, as both Augustine[4] and Gregory[5] say. Therefore neither can anyone see the truth by himself unless his mind is newly illumined by God.

3.    Just as the bodily eye is related to seeing bodies, so the intellect is related to perceiving intelligible truth. This is clear in the treatise *On the Soul*.[6] But the bodily eye cannot see bodies without the additional illumination of the corporeal sun. Therefore neither can the human intellect see the truth without being illumined by the light of the invisible Sun, who is God.

4.    Actions are said to be in our power if we have adequate principles within us to exercise them. But it is not in our power to know the truth, for at times many try to know the truth but are unable to know it. Consequently we do not have sufficient principles within us to know the truth. Therefore it is necessary to receive outside help to know it; and so the previous conclusion follows.

5.    The activity of the human mind is more dependent on the divine light than the activity of a lower sensible creature on the light of a heavenly body. But even though lower bodies have forms which are the principles of natural activities, nevertheless they cannot complete their operations unless they are aided by the additional light of the

---

illumination, see E. Gilson, *The Christian Philosophy of St. Thomas Aquinas*, pp. 185, 214-215, 217-219, 362-364. On the general problem of divine illumination in the Middle Ages, see E. Gilson, *The Spirit of Mediaeval Philosophy*, ch. 12, 13; idem, "Pourquoi s. Thomas a critiqué s. Augustin," *Archives d'histoire doctrinale et littéraire du moyen âge* 1 (1926), 5-127: M. Grabmann, *Die theol. Erkenntnis- und Einleitungslehre des hl. Thomas von Aquin;* L. Elders, *Faith and Science*, pp. 25-30.

3    Aristotle, *Nicomachean Ethics* 1.2 (1095b10).
4    St. Augustine, *De magistro* 12.40 and 14.45 CCL 29: 197-199 and 201-202.
5    St. Gregory, *Homilia* 30.3, PL 76:1222A.
6    Aristotle, *De anima* 3.4 (429a16-18).

sun and stars. Thus Dionysius[7] states that the light of the sun "contributes to the generation of sensible bodies and brings them to life and nourishes and increases them." Consequently, in order for the human mind to see the truth, neither is the natural light (which is in a way its form) sufficient, unless another light is added, namely the divine light.

6.    In all causes arranged in an essential, and not in an accidental order, the effect does not come from the secondary cause except through the activity of the first cause, as is clear in the *Book on Causes*.[8] But the human mind is placed under the uncreated light in an essential and not in an accidental order. Consequently the operation of the mind that is its proper effect, namely knowing the truth, cannot come from it without the activity of the primary uncreated light, and its activity seems to be nothing but illumination. And so the above conclusion follows.

7.    The will has the same relation to right willing as the intellect has to correct thinking. But the will cannot will rightly unless helped by divine grace, as Augustine says.[9] Therefore, neither can the intellect understand the truth unless it is illumined by the divine light.

8.    We are not blamed for ascribing to our powers that for which our powers suffice, like running or building. But it is blameworthy for someone to attribute knowledge of the truth to his own natural powers. In fact, on the contrary, we are told to ascribe it to God, as Ecclesiasticus says 51:23: "To him who gives me wisdom I will give glory." Hence our powers are not adequate to know the truth; and so the same conclusion follows as before.

*On the contrary*, the human mind is divinely illumined by a natural light, according to Psalm 4:7: "The light of your countenance, O Lord, is signed upon us." Therefore, if this light, because it is created, is not adequate to know the truth, but needs a new illumination, the added light with equal reason will not suffice, but will require another light, and so on to infinity— a process that can never be completed. And so it will be impossible to know any truth. Therefore

[7] Pseudo-Dionysius, *De divinis nominibus* 4.4, PG 3:700A.
[8] *Liber de causis*, prop. 1, ed. Bardenhewer, n. 1, p. 164.15-18.
[9] St. Augustine, *Contra duas epistolas Pelagianorum* 1.3.7, PL 44:553.

we must depend on the first light, so that the human mind can see the truth by its natural light without anything being added.

2. Just as an actually visible object suffices to activate sight, so an actually intelligible object suffices to activate the intellect, if it is proportionate [to the intellect]. But our mind has within it the power to make objects actually intelligible, namely the agent intellect, and an intelligible object of this sort is proportionate to the intellect. So the mind does not need a new illumination in order to know the truth.

3. Intellectual light is related to mental sight as physical light is to bodily sight. But every physical light, no matter how weak, makes something be seen physically—at least itself. Therefore the intellectual light that is connatural to the mind also suffices to know some truth.

4. All works of art depend on the knowledge of some truth, for they originate in knowledge. But according to Augustine free choice, taken in itself, is capable of some works of art, for example, building houses and the like. Therefore the mind suffices for knowing some truth without a new divine illumination.

*Reply:* The active and passive powers [of the soul] differ in that the passive ones cannot actually exercise their specific activity unless they are moved by their active [counterparts]; for example, a sense cannot perceive unless it is stimulated by a sensible object. But the active powers can operate without being moved by anything else, as is clear in the case of the powers of the vegetative soul.

Now there are two kinds of intellectual powers: one that is active, namely the agent intellect, and one that is passive, namely the possible intellect. Some held that only the possible intellect was a power of the soul; the agent intellect was a certain separate substance. This is the opinion of Avicenna.[10] The consequence of this view is that the human soul is incapable of actually exercising its specific activity, which is knowing the truth, unless it is illumined by the external light of that separate substance which he calls the agent intellect.

But the words of the Philosopher in *On the Soul*[11] would rather seem to mean that the agent intellect is a power of the soul. The

---

[10] Avicenna, *De anima* 5.5, ed. Van Riet 2:126-127. See St. Thomas, *Contra gentiles* 2.76.
[11] Aristotle, *De anima* 3.5 (430a10-15).

authority of sacred Scripture[12] is also in agreement with this, teaching as it does that we are marked with an intelligible light, to which the Philosopher likens the agent intellect. Consequently both an active and a passive power are ascribed to the soul in its intellectual activity, which is knowing the truth. So, just as the other natural active powers, joined to their passive counterparts suffice for natural activities, so also the soul, endowed with an active and passive power, is adequate for the perception of truth.

Every created active power, however, is finite, and so its adequacy is restricted to limited effects. It is incapable of other effects unless a new power is added. Thus there are some intelligible truths to which the efficacy of the agent intellect extends, like the principles we naturally know and the conclusions we deduce from them. In order to know them we do not need a new intellectual light; the light endowed by nature suffices. There are some truths, however, which do not come within the range of these principles, like the truths of faith, which transcend the faculty of reason, also future contingents and other matters of this sort. The human mind cannot know these without being divinely illumined by a new light supplementing the natural light.

Though an additional new light is unnecessary for a knowledge of whatever comes within the reach of natural reason, the divine activity is nevertheless required. Besides the act by which God establishes the natures of things, giving to all of them their forms and specific powers by which they can exercise their activities, he also accomplishes the works of providence in things by directing and moving the powers of all of them to their specific acts.[13] Thus every creature is subject to the divine governance, as instruments come under the control of the artist[14] and natural qualities are subject to the powers of the nutritive soul, as is said in *On the Soul*.[15] Just as digestion is a consequence of natural heat, following the law that the digestive power imposes upon heat, and all the powers of sublunar bodies operate in accordance with the movement and direction of

---

[12] Psalm 4:7.
[13] See St. Thomas, *Summa theol.* 1.105.5.
[14] See St. Thomas, *Contra gentiles* 3.67.
[15] Aristotle, *De anima* 2.4 (416b27-29).

the powers of the heavenly bodies, so all created active powers function under the movement and direction of the creator. It follows that the human mind needs the divine activity in all knowledge of the truth, but in knowing natural things it does not require a new light but only the divine movement and direction; but in knowing other matters it needs in addition a new illumination. And because Boethius is here speaking of the latter, he says "to the extent that the divine light has deigned to enkindle the spark of my mind."[16]

*Replies to Opposing Arguments:*

*Reply to 1.* Though by ourselves, without the divine activity, we are insufficient to think of anything, a new light need not be communicated to us in all our knowledge.

*Reply to 2.* God teaches us interiorly in the case of natural objects of knowledge by creating a natural light within us and by directing it to the truth, but also in other matters by imparting to us a new light.

*Reply to 3.* When the eye of the body is illuminated by the corporeal sun, it does not acquire a light connatural to itself by which it can make things actually visible, as our mind does from the illumination of the uncreated Sun. So the eye always needs an exterior light, but the mind does not.

*Reply to 4.* Where the intelligible light is pure, as in the angels, it discloses without difficulty everything naturally knowable, in such a way that they can know all natural truths. In us, however, the intelligible light is darkened by its union with the body and the bodily powers, and this hinders it so that it cannot readily grasp the truth that is even naturally knowable. As Wisdom (9:15) says: "for a perishable body weighs down the soul, and this earthly tent burdens the thoughtful mind." These obstacles are the reason why it is not entirely in our power to know the truth. But everyone has the capacity to do so to a greater or lesser extent, depending on the purity of his intelligible light.

*Reply to 5.* Though sublunar bodies need to be moved by heavenly bodies in order to operate, they do not have to receive new forms from them in order to fulfill their specific activities. Similarly, it is

---

[16] See above, p. 7.

not necessary that the human mind, which is moved by God to know things naturally knowable, be flooded with a new light.

*Reply to 6.*   As Augustine says,[17] just as air is illuminated by the presence of light, which in its absence leaves air in continual darkness, so also the mind is illuminated by God. God is always the cause of the soul's natural light—not different lights but one and the same. He is the cause not only of its coming into existence but of its existence itself. In this way, therefore, God is constantly at work in the mind, endowing it with its natural light and giving it direction. So the mind, as it goes about its work, does not lack the activity of the first cause.

*Reply to 7.*   The will can never will the good without the divine impulse; but it can will the good without the influx of grace, but in this case it does not merit. Similarly, the intellect cannot know any truth without being moved by God; but, except for those truths that surpass natural knowledge, it can do so without an influx of new light.

*Reply to 8.*   Because God causes the natural light within us by conserving it, and directs it in order that it might see, it is clear that the perception of truth should principally be ascribed to him, as the activity of an art is more attributable to the workman than to his saw.

ARTICLE TWO

*Can the Human Mind Arrive at a Knowledge of God?*[1]

*We proceed to the second article as follows:*

It seems that it is impossible for us to know God.

*1.*   For we have no way of knowing what remains unknown to us at the peak of our knowledge. But at the highest point of our knowledge we are united to God only as to one who is, as it were, unknown, as Dionysius states.[2] In no way, therefore, can we know God.

---

[17] St. Augustine, *De Genesi ad litteram* 8.12, CSEL 28 (sect. 3, pt. 2), pp. 250.2-5.

[1] See St. Thomas, *Sent.* 1, d. 3, q. 1, a. 1 and 3; *Summa theol.* 1.12.1.

[2] Pseudo-Dionysius, *Mystica theologia* 1.3, PG 3:1001A.

2. Everything that is known is known through some form. But, as Augustine says,[3] God eludes every form of our understanding. Hence there is no way for us to know him.

3. There must be some proportion between the knower and the knowable object, as there must be between any power and its object. But there can be no proportion between our intellect and God, as there can be none between the finite and the infinite.[4] Therefore our intellect can in no way know God.

4. Because potency and act are in the same genus, dividing as they do all the genera of being, no power can issue into an act that is outside its genus. The senses, for example, cannot know intelligible substance. But God is outside every genus.[5] Therefore he cannot be known by any intellect that is in a genus. But this is the nature of our intellect. The conclusion follows.

5. If you take away the first, you remove everything that follows. But the first intelligible object is the essence of a thing. Thus in *On the Soul*[6] it is said that essence is the proper object of the intellect, and it is by means of essence that we demonstrate a thing's existence and all its other features.[7] But we cannot know what God is, as Damascene says.[8] Hence we can know nothing about him.

*On the contrary*, it is said in Romans 1:20: "Ever since the creation of the world his invisible nature, namely his eternal power and deity, has been clearly perceived in the things that have been made."

2. Jeremiah 9:24 says: "Let him who glories glory in this, that he understands and knows me." But this glory would be empty if we could not know him. Therefore we can know God.

---

[3] This saying has not been found in the works of St. Augustine. It is implied in his *Enarrationes in Psalmos*, on Ps. 85: 8 and 144:3, CCL 39:1186 and CCL 40:2090-2091.

[4] See St. Thomas, *Summa theol.* 1.2.2, arg. 3 and reply.

[5] See Q. 6, a. 3, ed. Decker, p. 222.6, trans. Maurer, p. 85.

[6] Aristotle, *De anima* 3.6 (430b28).

[7] See Aristotle, *Post. Anal.* 1.8 (75b31), 2.10 (94a11-14); *De anima* 1.1 (402b25).

[8] St. John Damascene, *De fide orthodoxa* 1.2 and 4, ed. Buytaert, p. 15.40-45 and 19.3-5, 20.33.

3. Nothing is loved unless it is known, as Augustine explains.[9] But we are commanded to love God. Therefore we can know him, for we are not ordered to do the impossible.

*Reply:* Something can be known in two ways: in one way through its own form, as the eye sees a stone through the likeness of a stone; in another way through the form of something else similar to itself, as a cause is known through the likeness of its effect and a man through the form of his image. In turn, something is seen through its own form in two ways: first, through the form which is the reality itself, as God knows himself through his essence and also as an angel knows himself. Second, through a form derived from the reality, whether it be abstracted from it, as when the form is more immaterial than the reality, for example, as the form of a stone is abstracted from the stone; or whether it be implanted in the intelligence by the reality, as when the reality is simpler than the likeness through which it is known, as Avicenna[10] says we know the Intelligences through notions they implant in us. Now, because our intellect in its present state has a definite relationship to forms that are abstracted from the senses, being related to images as sight to colors, as the treatise *On the Soul* says,[11] in its present state it cannot know God through the form that is his essence, but the blessed will know him in this way in heaven. For any likeness imprinted by him in the human mind would be insufficient to make it know his essence because it infinitely transcends every created form. Consequently, as Augustine says,[12] God cannot be accessible to the intellect through created forms. Neither in the present life do we know God through purely intelligible forms that bear some likeness to him; this is because of the natural relation of our intellect to images mentioned above.

It remains that God is known only through the form of his effect. Now effects are of two kinds. One is equal to the power of its cause, and through an effect of this sort the power— and consequently the essence—of the cause is fully known. The other effect falls short

---

[9] St. Augustine, *De Trinitate* 8.4.6 and 13.20.26, CCL 50:274-275 and 419.

[10] Avicenna, *De anima* 5.5, ed. Van Riet 2: 126-127. See St. Thomas, *Summa theol.*1.84.4.

[11] Aristotle, *De anima* 3.7 (431a14).

[12] See above, p. 20, n. 3.

of the above-mentioned equality, and through such an effect the power of the agent cannot be fully grasped and consequently neither can its essence: we only know that the cause exists (*quod est*). And so knowledge of the effect functions as the principle of knowing that a cause exists (*an est*), as the essence of the cause itself does when it is known through its form. Now all effects stand in this relation to God. It follows that in the present life we can only come to know that he exists (*quia est*). Nevertheless, among those knowing that he exists, the knowledge of one is more perfect than that of another, because a cause is more perfectly known from its effect to the degree that the relation of the cause to the effect is more perfectly apprehended.

Now we can consider from three points of view the relation in an effect that falls short of equality with its cause: with respect to the coming forth of the effect from the cause, with respect to the effect acquiring a likeness to its cause, and with respect to its falling short of perfectly acquiring it. So the human mind advances in three ways in knowing God, though it does not reach a knowledge of what he is (*quid est*), but only that he is (*an est*).[13] First, by knowing more perfectly his power in producing things. Second, by knowing him as the cause of more lofty effects which, because they bear some resemblance to him, give more praise to his greatness. Third, by an ever-growing knowledge of him as distant from everything that appears in his effects. Thus Dionysius says that we know God as the cause of all things, by transcendence and by negation.[14]

The human mind receives its greatest help in this advance of knowledge when its natural light is strengthened by a new illumination, like the light of faith and the gifts of wisdom and understanding, through which the mind is said to be raised above itself in contemplation, inasmuch as it knows that God is above everything it naturally comprehends. But because it is not competent to penetrate to a vision of

[13] For the distinction between knowledge *quid est* and *quia est*, see also Aristotle, *Post. Anal.* 2. 7-10; St. Thomas, *In Post. Anal.* 2, lect. 1, n. 8; Q. 6, a.3, ed. Decker, pp. 220-222, trans. Maurer, pp. 82-86. *Contra gentiles* 1.30 and 3.49; *De potentia* 7.5; *De veritate* 2.1, ad 9. See also E. Gilson, *The Christian Philosophy of St. Thomas Aquinas*, pp. 103-110; J. Maritain, *The Degrees of Knowledge*, pp. 422-429; A. C. Pegis, "Penitus Manet Ignotum," *Mediaeval Studies* 27 (1965), 212-226; J. F. Wippel, *Metaphysical Themes in Thomas Aquinas*, ch. 9.

[14] Pseudo-Dionysius *De divinis nominibus* 7.3, PG 3: 869D-872A.

his essence, it is said in a way to be turned back upon itself by a superior light. This is what Gregory says,[15] glossing the text of Genesis 32:30: "I have seen God face to face": "When the eye of the soul turns to God, it recoils at the flash of infinity."

*Replies to Opposing Arguments:*

*Reply to 1.* We are said to know God as unknown at the highest point of our knowledge because we find that the mind has made the greatest advance in knowledge when it knows that his essence transcends everything it can apprehend in the present life. Thus, although what he is (*quid est*) remains unknown, that he is (*quia est*) is nonetheless known.

*Reply to 2.* From the fact that God eludes every form of the intellect, it appears that what he is (*quid est*) cannot be known, but, as has been said, only that he is (*an est*).

*Reply to 3.* Proportion is nothing else than a relation of two things coming together with each other in some respect, whether this be by agreement or difference. Things can be understood to agree in two ways: first, from the fact that they belong to the same genus of quantity or quality, like the relation of surface to surface or of number to number, insofar as one is greater than the other or equal to it, or the relation of one heat to another. In this sense there can be no proportion between God and creatures because they do not share a common genus. Second, things can be understood to agree from the fact that they fit into some order. In this sense we understand the proportion between matter and form, maker and thing made, and other things of this sort. This kind of proportion is needed between the knowing power and the knowable object, because the knowable object is a sort of actuality of the knowing power. And in this sense there is also a proportion of creatures to God, as the effect to its cause and the knower to the knowable object. However, owing to the infinite transcendence of the creator over the creature, there is no proportion of the creature to the creator such that the creature receives the full power of his influence or knows him perfectly, as he perfectly knows himself.

---

[15] *Glossa ordinaria* 1, col. 356D. See St. Gregory the Great, *Moralia* 24.6.12, CCL 143B: 1196.

*Reply to 4.* The intellect and the intelligible object are in the same genus as potency and act. God, however, is not in the genus of intelligible objects as though he were included under the genus, that it, as participating the nature of the genus, but he does belong to the genus as its principle. Moreover, his effects are not outside the genus of intelligible objects, and so he can be known in this life through his effects and in heaven through his essence. Besides, the term "intelligible" seems to be negative rather than affirmative, for anything is intelligible from the fact that it is free or separated from matter. Now negative terms are true of God, while affirmative terms are inexact, as Dionysius says.[16]

*Reply to 5.* When something is not known through its form but through its effect, the form of the effect takes the place of the form of the thing itself, for from the effect itself it is known that the cause exists.

### ARTICLE THREE

### *Is God What the Mind First Knows?*[1]

*We proceed to the third article as follows:*

It seems that God is what the mind first knows.

*1.* For we know first that in which everything else is known and through which we judge about everything we know, as the eye perceives light before it perceives what is seen by means of light, and the intellect knows principles before conclusions. But everything is known in the first truth, and we judge everything by means of it, as Augustine says.[2] Therefore what we know first is the first truth, namely God.

*2.* When there are several causes arranged in order, the first cause has a greater influence on the effect than the second cause,

---

[16] Pseudo-Dionysius, *De caelesti hierarchia* 2.3, PG 3:141A.

[1] See St. Thomas, *Sent.* 1, d. 3, q. 1, a. 2; *De veritate* 10.12; *Contra gentiles* 1.10-11; *Summa theol.* 1.2.1, 1.88.3.

[2] St. Augustine, *De Trinitate* 9.7.12 and 12.2.2, CCL 50:300-304 and 2, 356-357. *De vera religione* 31.57, CCL 32:224.

and it is the last to leave it, according to the *Book on Causes*.[3] Now, because human knowledge is caused by realities, the knowable or intelligible is the cause of the human mind's understanding. Consequently the first of all intelligibles has the primary influence on it. But the effect of an intelligible on the intellect as such is that it be understood. Hence God, who is the primary intelligible, is first known by our intellect.

*3.* In all our knowledge, in which what is prior and simpler is first known, we know before all else what is first and most simple. Now it seems that what is prior and simpler precedes everything else in presenting themselves to human knowledge, for being is that which is first given to human knowledge, as Avicenna says.[4] Now, "Being is the first of created things."[5] God, therefore, who is absolutely first and most simple, first offers himself to human knowledge.

*4.* The end comes first in our intention but last in being carried into effect. Now God is the final end of the human will, all other ends being directed to it. Hence he is first in being intended. But this is impossible unless he is known. Therefore God offers himself first to our knowledge.

*5.* That which needs no previous handling in order to be worked upon by an agent comes under the activity of that agent before that which requires some other operation; for example, wood that is already cut is subject to the activity of the maker of a bench before uncut wood. Now sensible things need to be abstracted from matter by the agent intellect before they are understood by the possible intellect. But God in himself is most removed from matter. Therefore he is known by the possible intellect before sensible things.

*6.* The first objects of our knowledge are things which we naturally know and which cannot be thought not to be. But the knowledge of God's existence is naturally implanted in everyone, as Damascene says.[6] Moreover, God cannot be thought not to exist, as Anselm states.[7] Hence what we know first of all is God.

---

[3] *Liber de causis*, prop. 1, ed. Bardenhewer, p. 163.6-8, 164.12-15.
[4] Avicenna, *Metaphysics* 1.5, ed. Van Riet 1:31-32.2-4.
[5] See *Liber de causis*, prop. 4, ed cit., p. 166.19.
[6] St. John Damascene, *De fide orthodoxa* 1.1, ed. Buytaert, 12.22.
[7] St. Anselm, *Proslogion* 3, ed. Schmitt, p. 103.3.

*On the contrary*, according to the Philosopher[8] all our knowledge begins from the senses. Now God is furthest removed from the senses. Therefore we do not know him first, but last.

2. According to the Philosopher[9] what is posterior in the order of nature is prior in relation to us, and what is less known in the order of nature is better known to us. But creatures are by nature posterior to and less known than God. Therefore to us the knowledge of God comes later.

3. What is promised as our final reward is not first, preceding all merits. But the knowledge of God is promised to us as the final reward of all our knowledge and action. Therefore God is not known to us first.

*Reply:* Some[10] have asserted that even in this life what the human mind first knows is God himself, who is the first truth, and everything else is known through him. But this appears to be false, because man's beatitude is knowing God through his essence, and so, if it were true, it would follow that everyone would be perfectly happy. Moreover, because all the perfections attributed to his essence are one in that essence, no one would be in error about the attributes of God, which is shown by experience to be patently false. Furthermore, what the mind first knows must be most certain, and consequently the mind is sure that it understands it; but this is not so in the present case. This opinion is also contrary to the authority of Scripture which says in Exodus 33:20: "Man will not see me and live."

Others[11] have claimed that what we first know in this life is not the divine essence but the influx of its light, and in this way what

---

[8] Aristotle, *Post. Anal.* 2.19 (1003-11, b 3-5).

[9] Aristotle, ibid., 1.2 (71b33-72a5); *Phys.* 1.1 (184a16-21); *Metaph.* 7.4 (1029b3-12); *Nic. Ethics* 1.2 (1095b2).

[10] The identity of these theologians is unknown. See M. Grabmann, *Die theol. Erkenntnis- und Einleitungslehre des hl. Thomas von Aquin...*, pp. 76-80; L. Elders, *Faith and Science*, p. 36.

[11] See William of Auvergne (d. 1249), for whom "the creator himself is the natural and appropriate book of the human mind." *De anima* 7.6, pp. 211-212. See also Bonaventure (d. 1274), who followed Augustine in holding that God, as the supreme light, is the object most knowable to the human soul. He is known through the influence of the soul's connatural light, which is an infused likeness of God, and in this sense God is the first object knowable to the human intellect. See Bonaventure, *Sent.*, 1, d. 3, pt. 1, a. un. q. 1, con. 2, and 2, d. 3, pt. 2, a. 2, q. 2, ad 4, ed. Quaracchi 1:68, and 2:123. See J. F. Quinn, *The Historical Constitution of St. Bonaventure's Philosophy*, pp. 430-435.

we first know is God. But neither can this be defended, because the first light divinely implanted in the mind is the natural light that forms our intellectual faculty. Now this light is not what is first known by the mind, either in the sense that we know what it is (*quid est*) for we need a lengthy inquiry to know the nature of the intellect, or in the sense that we know that it exists (*an est*), for we are only aware of our having an intellect by being conscious of our understanding, as the Philosopher explains in the *Ethics*.[12] Now no one understands that he understands unless he understands something intelligible. Clearly, then, the knowledge of something intelligible comes before the knowledge by which we know that we understand, and consequently before the knowledge by which we know that we have an intellect. It follows that the influx of the natural intelligible light cannot be that which we first know, and much less any other influx of light.

Our answer to the question is that "what we first know" can have two meanings: (1) with reference to the order of the different powers [of the soul], (2) with reference to the order of the objects in one power. In the first sense, because all our intellect's knowledge is derived from the senses, what is perceptible by the senses is known to us before what is knowable by the intellect, that is to say, the singular or sensible intelligible. In the second sense, what is primarily knowable to each power is its proper object. Now, in the human intellect there is an active and a passive power. The object of the passive power, or possible intellect, will be that which is produced by the active power, or agent intellect, because a passive power ought to have its own active [counterpart]. Now the agent intellect does not render separated forms intelligible, which are in fact intelligible of themselves, but rather forms that it abstracts from images. Therefore objects of this sort are first known by our intellect.

Among these objects those are prior that first present themselves to the abstracting intellect. They are the ones that are inclusive of more items, either as a universal whole or as an integral whole.[13] Hence the intellect first knows the more universal, and it knows

---

[12] Aristotle, *Nic. Ethics* 9.9 (1170a31-b1). See St. Thomas, *De veritate* 10.8.
[13] On universal and integral wholes, see St. Thomas, *Sent.* 1, d. 19, q. 4, a. 1 and 2; *Summa theol.* 1.77.1, ad 1ᵐ.

composites before their constituent parts, for example the thing defined
before the parts of its definition. And because the senses bear a
certain resemblance to the intellect (for they also are receptive of
objects abstracted in a way from matter),[14] even the senses first know
more common particulars, for example this body before this animal.
So it is clear that it is absolutely impossible that what we first know
are God and the other separate substances. Rather, they are known
from other things, as is said in Romans 1:20: "Ever since the creation
of the world his invisible nature, namely his eternal power and deity,
has been clearly perceived in the things that have been made."

*Replies to Opposing Arguments:*

*Reply to 1.* From these and similar words of Augustine we are
not to understand that the uncreated truth itself is the proximate
principle by which we understand and judge, but that we know and
judge through its likeness implanted in us. This light has no power
except from the primary light, as in demonstrations secondary principles
are certain only because of primary principles. The implanted light
itself need not be the first object of our knowledge, for by it we do
not know other things as by an object of knowledge serving as a
medium of knowledge, but as by that which makes other things
knowable.[15] So it is not necessary that it be known except in the
knowable objects themselves, as light need not be what the eye first
sees, except in the illuminated color itself.

*Reply to 2.* The influence on the final effect of all causes arranged
in order is not of the same kind. Hence it is not necessary that the
primary intelligible object influence our intellect in such a way that
it be understood, but that it bestow the power of understanding. Or
the reply might be given that, although God is absolutely first in the
line of intelligible beings, he is not first in the line of beings intelligible
to us.

*Reply to 3.* Though we first know the primary objects of the
kind the intellect abstracts from images, like being and one, it is not
necessary that we first know those which are absolutely primary,

---

[14] See St. Thomas, *In De anima* 2.3, lect. 5, n. 284; 3.8, lect. 13, n. 792 and
3.12, lect. 17, n. 850.
[15] See St. Thomas, *Summa theol.* 1.84.5, and 88.3, ad 1ᵐ.

which, unlike these, are not included in the notion of its proper object.

*Reply to 4.*    Though God is the final end to be reached and first in the intention of our natural desire, it is not necessary that he be first in the knowledge of the human mind which is directed to the end, but in the knowledge of the one who does the directing, just as in the case of other agents which tend to their end by natural desire. However, he is known and desired in a general way from the very beginning, inasmuch as the mind longs to be well and to live well, which is possible for it only when it possesses God.

*Reply to 5.*    Though the separate substances do not need to be abstracted in order to be understood, nevertheless they are not intelligible through the light of the agent intellect. So they are not the primary objects of our intellect, for what is intelligible through this light is the object of the intellect, just as what is visible through physical light is the object of sight.

*Reply to 6.*    Taken in itself, God's existence is self-evident, because his essence is his existence (*esse*) (this is Anselm's way of speaking),[16] but it is not evident to us who do not see his essence. However, we are said to have an innate knowledge of him insofar as we can easily perceive that he exists by means of principles implanted in us by nature.

ARTICLE FOUR

*Is the Human Mind by Itself Able to Arrive at a Knowledge of the Divine Trinity?*[1]

*We proceed to the fourth article as follows:*

It seems that the mind is capable of knowing the divine Trinity by natural reason.

*1.*    For whatever pertains to being as being must especially be found in the first being. Now the condition of being three pertains

---

[16] See above, note 7. St. Thomas interprets St. Anselm to mean that God's existence is self-evident. See *Sent.* 1, d. 3, q. 1, a. 2, arg. 4; *Summa theol.* 1.2.1, arg. 2 and reply.

[1] See St. Thomas, *Sent.* 1, d. 3, q. 1, a. 4; *De veritate* 10.13; *Summa theol.* 1.32.1.

to being as being because it is found in all beings; as Augustine says,[2] everything has measure, beauty and order. Therefore it can be known by natural reason that God is threefold.

2.    No perfection is to be denied to God. But three is the number of the perfection of all things, as is said in the book *On the Heavens and Earth*.[3] Therefore trinity should be ascribed to God, and so the same conclusion follows as before.

3.    All inequality can be reduced to a prior equality, as multitude to unity.[4] Now there is inequality between God and the first created being. Therefore there must be some prior equality; and since this can only belong to a multitude, there must be some plurality in God.

4.    All equivocity can be reduced to univocity. Now the procession of creatures from God is equivocal.[5] Therefore prior to this we must affirm an univocal procession by which God proceeds from God, and from this follows the Trinity of persons.

5.    There can be no joyous possession of any good without fellowship. Now from eternity God possesses the good with the greatest joy. Therefore he has an eternal fellowship, and this can only be the fellowship of the divine persons, because no creature is eternal. So we must posit several persons in the deity.

6.    It can be proved by natural reason that God knows. But from the fact that he knows it follows that he conceives a word, for this is common to everyone who knows. Therefore it can be known by natural reason that there is a generation of the Son, and for the same reason a procession of love.

7.    Richard of St. Victor says[6]: "I believe without any doubt, because in giving an account of anything whose existence is necessary, not only probable but also necessary arguments are not wanting." Now it is necessary that God be threefold and one because he is eternal. Consequently there are also necessary reasons for this. And so the previous conclusion follows.

[2] St. Augustine, *De natura boni* 3, CSEL 25: 856.9-21.
[3] Aristotle, *De caelo* 1.1 (268a9-13).
[4] See Boethius, *De institutione arithmetica* 2.1, p. 77.9-21.
[5] See Seneca, *Epistula* 6.4.
[6] Richard of St. Victor, *De Trinitate* 1.4, PL 196: 892C.

*8.* The Platonists[7] knew about God only by reason. But they themselves posited at least two persons: God the Father and a Mind begotten by him containing the ideas of all things, which we affirm of the Son. Therefore a plurality of persons can be known by natural reason.

*9.* The Philosopher says:[8] "By this number [three] we have shown that we ourselves praise God the creator." So the above conclusion holds.

*10.* In the present life we can have absolutely no knowledge of what God is (*quid est*), but only that he exists (*an est*). Now in some way, namely by faith, we know that God is three and one. Consequently this does not have to do with what God is but with his existence. But we can show by natural reason that God exists. Therefore it can also be known by natural reason that God is three and one.

*On the contrary,* faith concerns what is not apparent to reason, as is clear from Hebrews 11:1. Now it is an article of faith that God is three and one. Therefore reason is not adequate to perceive this.

2. All natural reason gets its power from the first principles that it knows naturally. But the fact that God is three and one cannot be deduced from naturally known principles, which are drawn from the senses, because in the sensible world we find nothing similar to there being three persons with one essence. Consequently it cannot be known by reason that God is three and one.

3. Ambrose says[9]: "It is impossible for me to know the mystery of the divine birth; the mind fails, the voice is silent, and not only mine but also the angels'." Therefore natural reason is not adequate to know the divine birth, and consequently neither the Trinity of persons.

*Reply:* That God is both threefold and one is solely an object of belief. There is no way of proving it demonstratively, though some arguments can be given in its favor which are not necessarily convincing nor very probable, except to the believer. This is evident from the fact that in the present life we know God only from his

---

[7] See Q. 3, a. 4, below, p. 80.

[8] Aristotle, *De caelo* 1.1 (268a14).

[9] St. Ambrose, *De fide* 1.10.64, PL 16: 565D-566A.

effects, as can be shown from what has been said above.[10] Therefore through natural reason we can know about God only what we grasp of him from the relation his effects bear to him, for example, attributes that designate his causality and his transcendence over his effects, and that deny of him the imperfections of his effects. Now the Trinity of persons cannot be known from the divine causality itself, because causality belongs in common to the whole Trinity. Neither is it expressed in negative terms. Consequently it is absolutely impossible to give a demonstrative proof that God is threefold and one.

*Replies to Opposing Arguments:*

*Reply to 1.* Things that are multiple in creatures are really one in God. Consequently, though a trinity may be found in every creature, it cannot necessarily be deduced from this that there is a trinity in God, except in concept, and this plurality is not sufficient to distinguish the persons.

*Reply to 2.* We find threeness as a perfection in God even if we consider his unity in essence: not that his essence itself is numbered, but because it virtually contains the perfection of all numbers, as Boethius says.[11]

*Reply to 3.* Even apart from the distinction of persons there is equality in God inasmuch as his power is equal to his wisdom. Another possible reply is that there are two factors to consider in equality: the plurality of subjects (*suppositorum*) which are related to each other, and the unity of quantity, which is the cause of equality. Therefore inequality is reduced to equality, not by reason of the plurality of subjects (*suppositorum*), but by reason of the cause, because just as unity is the cause of equality, so plurality is the cause of inequality. So it is necessary that the cause of equality be prior to the cause of inequality. Not that there are equal items prior to all unequal ones; otherwise among numbers there would have to be something before unity and duality, which are unequal, or plurality would be present in unity itself.

*Reply to 4.* Though all equivocity is reducible to univocity, equivocal generation need not be reduced to univocal generation, but to a producer which is univocal in itself. For we see in nature that

---

[10] See above, Q. 1, a. 2, pp. 21-22.
[11] Boethius, *De institutione arithmetica* 2.8, p. 93.7-9.

equivocal generations are prior to univocal ones, because equivocal causes exercise an influence over a whole species, whereas the influence of univocal causes is limited to one individual. Hence they are as it were instruments of equivocal causes, as sublunar bodies are so to speak instruments of the heavenly bodies.[12]

*Reply to 5.* A person cannot live a happy life without fellowship because he is not entirely self-sufficient. This is why animals which are self-sufficient as individuals do not need a common life, but live alone. Now God is most self-sufficient. Consequently, even aside from the distinction of persons he is most perfectly joyful.

*Reply to 6.* In God, knower and object known are identical. Therefore, from the fact that he is a knower it is not necessary to posit in him a conceived object, really distinct from himself, as is the case with us. But the Trinity of persons calls for a real distinction.

*Reply to 7.* The interpretation of that sentence is clear from the sequel: "though, despite our efforts, they may elude us." Everything necessary in itself is either self-evident or knowable through something else but it need not be so in relation to us. So we are not able by our own effort to discover a necessary argument to prove all necessary truths.

*Reply to 8.* In fact, the position of the Platonists has no bearing on the present issue, though verbally it may seem to. The Platonists did not claim that that Mind had the same essence as God the Father, but that it was another immaterial substance proceeding from him; and they affirmed a third soul of the world, as is clear from Macrobius.[13] Because they called all immaterial substances gods, they said that these are three gods, as Augustine states.[14] Since they did not posit anything similar to the Holy Spirit, as they did to the Father and the Son (the world soul is not a bond uniting the other two, in their view, as the Holy Spirit is the bond of the Father and Son), they are said to have been wanting in the third figure, that is, in the knowledge of the third person.[15]

---

[12] On univocal and equivocal causes, see *Summa theol.* 1.4.3 and 1.6.2.

[13] Macrobius, *Comm. in somnium Scipionis* 1.2.14-16 and 1.6.20, p. 482.9-28 and 499.18-20.

[14] St. Augustine, *De civitate Dei* 10.29, CCL 47:304.1-3.

[15] *Glossa ordinaria* 1, col. 555B. See Peter Lombard, *Glossa in Rom.* 1.20, PL 191:1328C-D; *Sent.* 1, d. 3, c. 1, n. 9, ed. Grottaferrata 1, pt. 2, p. 71.23-25.

We might also reply with the commonly held opinion that they knew two persons with their appropriated attributes of power and wisdom, but not with their proper attributes.[16] Now goodness, which is appropriated to the Holy Spirit, especially concerns effects of which they were ignorant.

*Reply to 9.* Aristotle did not mean that God was to be praised as three and one, but that, because of the perfection of the number three the ancients honored him with a threefold sacrifice and prayer.

*Reply to 10.* Everything that is in God is his one simple essence; but the perfections that are one in him are many in our intellect, and so our intellect can know one of them without the other. Consequently in our present state we cannot know about any one of them what it is (*quid est*), but only that it is (*an est*), and we can know the existence of one of them without knowing the existence of another; for example, if one knew that wisdom exists in God, but not that omnipotence exists in him. Similarly it can be known by natural reason that God exists, but not that he is threefold and one.

---

[16] See Peter Lombard, *Glossa in Rom.*, ibid., PL 191: 1329A.

# QUESTION TWO

# ON MAKING THE DIVINE KNOWLEDGE KNOWN[1]

There are four questions concerning this topic:

1. Is it permissible to make divine realities an object of investigation?
2. Can there be a science of divine realities?
3. Is it permissible to use philosophical arguments and authorities in the science of faith whose object is God?
4. Should divine realities be veiled by obscure and novel words?

ARTICLE ONE

*Is It Permissible to Make Divine Realities an Object of Investigation?*

*We proceed to the first article as follows:*

It does not seem right to inquire by reasoning into things divine.

*1.* For it is said in Ecclesiasticus 3:22: "Seek not what is too high for you, and search not into what is above your ability." But divine things especially are too high for us, and more particularly those held on faith. Therefore it is not permissible to investigate these matters.

*2.* Punishment is only inflicted for some fault. But, as is said in Proverbs 25:27: "He who is a searcher of majesty shall be overwhelmed by glory." Therefore it is not permitted to investigate thoroughly what belongs to the majesty of God.

*3.* Ambrose says[1]: "Away with arguments if you are looking for faith." But faith is necessary in divine things, especially concerning

---

[1] See St. Thomas, *Contra gentiles* 1.3.8.

[1] St. Ambrose, *De fide* 1.13.84, PL 16:570.

the Trinity. Therefore in this subject it is not permitted to investigate the truth by reasoning.

4. Speaking of generation in God, Ambrose says[2]: "It is not right to inquire into these high mysteries. One may know that the Son is begotten; it is not right to discuss how he is begotten." For the same reason, then, it is not permitted to inquire by means of arguments into anything connected with the Trinity.

5. As Gregory says[3], "Faith has no merit where human reason supplies proof." But it is wrong to do away with the merit of faith. Therefore it is not right to investigate matters of faith by reason.

6. All honor ought to be given to God. But secrets are to be respected by keeping silence about them. Thus Dionysius[4] speaks of "honoring by silence the hidden truth which is above us." This agrees with the words of Psalm 64:2, according to Jerome's text[5]: "Praise is silent before you, O God"; that is, silence itself is your praise. Therefore we ought to refrain in silence from inquiring into divine realities.

7. As the Philosopher says[6], no one can travel to infinity, because the purpose of every movement is to reach an end, which is not present in infinity. But God is infinitely remote from us. Now investigation is a kind of progression of reason toward the object under inquiry. So it seems that we ought not to inquire into divine realities.

On the contrary, we have the words of 1 Peter 3:15: "Always be prepared to make a defence to any one who calls you to account for the faith[7] that is in you." But this is impossible unless we inquire rationally into what we hold on faith. Therefore a rational investigation into matters of faith is necessary.

2. As Titus 1:9 says, it is the duty of a bishop "to give instruction in sound doctrine and also to confute those who contradict it." But

---

[2] Ibid., 1.10.65, PL 16: 566A.
[3] St. Gregory, *Hom.* 26.1, PL 76:1197C.
[4] Pseudo-Dionysius, *De caelesti hierarchia* 15.19, PG 3:340B.
[5] St. Jerome, *Liber psalmorum*, ps. 65, PL 28:1236C.
[6] Aristotle, *De caelo* 1.7 (274b11-13).
[7] The Greek text of the Bible reads "hope." St. Thomas follows a variant reading of the Vulgate. See L. Elders, *Faith and Science*, p. 42.

only by arguments can we refute those contradicting the faith. Therefore it is necessary to use reasoning in matters of faith.

3. Augustine says[8] that "with the help of the Lord our God we shall endeavor to give a reason for that very thing which they demand, namely that the Trinity is one God." Therefore we can use reasoning in inquiring into the Trinity.

4. Augustine says in his treatise against Felician[9]: "[Although in matters of faith it is easier to believe qualified testimony than to investigate by reasoning, nevertheless] because you not altogether unfittingly acknowledge both of these—since you do not omit to acknowledge testimony as well as the aforesaid reasoning—I am ready to proceed with you in this controversy on lines you have approved," that is, I shall use both reasoning and authority. Therefore the same conclusion follows.

*Reply*: Because our perfection consists in our union with God, we must have access to the divine to the fullest extent possible, using everything in our power, that our mind might be occupied with contemplation and our reason with the investigation of divine realities. As Psalm 72:28 says: "It is good for me to adhere to my God." So Aristotle[10] rejects the opinion of those who held that we should not meddle with what is divine, but only with what is human. "But we must not follow those," he says, "who advise us, being human, to think of human things, and, being mortal, of mortal things, but must, so far as we can, make ourselves immortal, and strain every nerve to live in accord with what is best in us."

In this regard, however, it is possible to go wrong in three ways. First, by presumption, delving into the divine in such a way that one tries to grasp it fully. This presumption is denounced in Job 11:7: "Can you search out the footprints of God and perfectly discover the Almighty?" Hilary also states:[11] "Do not plunge yourself into that mystery and secret of unimaginable birth. Do not immerse yourself in it, presuming to comprehend the heights of intelligence; rather, understand that they are incomprehensible."

---

[8] St. Augustine, *De Trinitate* 1.2.4, CCL 50:31.
[9] The treatise is in fact by Vigilius Thapsensis, *De unitate Trinitatis* 2, PL 42:1158.
[10] Aristotle, *Nic. Ethics* 10.7 (1177b31-34).
[11] St. Hilary, *De Trinitate* 2.10 and 11, CCL 62:48.11-13 and 49.14-16.

Second, one may err because in matters of faith he makes reason precede faith, instead of faith precede reason, as when someone is willing to believe only what he can discover by reason. It should in fact be just the opposite. Thus Hilary says[12]: "Begin by believing, inquire, press forward, persevere."

Third, by pursuing his speculation into the divine beyond the measure of his ability. Romans 12:3 says: "I bid every one of you not to be more wise than is necessary to be wise, but to be wise with sobriety, each according to the measure of faith that God has assigned him." For everyone has not been endowed in equal measure, so that what is beyond the ability of one is not beyond the ability of another.

*Replies to Opposing Arguments*

*Reply to 1.*    Those matters are said to be too high for us that go beyond our capacity, not those that are by nature of greater worth. For the more a person occupies himself with what is of greater value, provided that he keeps within the limits of his ability, the greater perfection he will reach. But should he exceed the measure of his ability even in the slightest matters, he easily falls into error. Thus the Gloss on Romans 12:3 says[13]: "Heretics are made in two ways: they fall into error and depart from the truth because they go beyond their limits when they concern themselves with the creator or with creatures."

*Reply to 2.*    To investigate thoroughly is, as it were, to conduct an inquiry to the very end. But it is unlawful and presumptuous for anyone to inquire into the divine as though he will reach the end of comprehending it.

*Reply to 3.*    Where faith is at stake there is no room for arguments opposed to faith or for those that attempt to precede it, but there is a place for those that in a due manner follow upon it.

*Reply to 4.*    It is not permitted to investigate the heavenly mysteries with the intention of fully comprehending them. This is clear from the words that follow: "One may know that the Son is begotten; it is not right to discuss how he is begotten." He who discusses the manner of that birth tries to know what that birth is, though we can know *that* divine realities are but not *what* they are.

---

[12] Ibid., 2. 10, CCL 62:48.13.
[13] *Glossa ordinaria* 3. col. 1994D.

*Reply to 5.*    There are two kinds of human reasoning. One is demonstrative, compelling the mind's assent. There can be no place in matters of faith for this kind of reasoning, but there can be in disproving claims that faith is impossible. For although matters of faith cannot be demonstratively proved, neither can they be demonstratively disproved. If this sort of reasoning were brought forward to prove what is held on faith, the merit of faith would be destroyed, because the assent to it would not be voluntary but necessary. But persuasive reasoning, drawn from analogies to the truths of faith, does not take away the nature of faith because it does not render them evident, for there is no reduction to first principles intuited by the mind. Neither does it deprive faith of its merit, because it does not compel the mind's assent but leaves the assent voluntary.

*Reply to 6.*    God is indeed respected by silence, but this does not mean that we may say nothing whatever about him, nor inquire into him, but that we should understand that however much we may say or inquire about him, we realize that we fall short of fully understanding him. Thus it is said in Ecclesiasticus 43:32: "When you praise the Lord, exalt him as much as you can; for he will surpass even that."

*Reply to 7.*    Since God is infinitely distant from creatures, no creature progresses toward God so as to equal him, either in what it receives from him or in knowing him. So the goal of the creature's progress is not something infinitely remote from the creature; but every creature is drawn to be more and more like God, as far as it is able.[14] So also the human mind should always be aroused to know more and more about God in the manner proper to it. Thus Hilary says:[15] "The person who with piety pursues the infinite may sometimes find it beyond his reach, but by advancing he makes progress."

ARTICLE TWO

*Can There Be a Science of Divine Realities?*[1]

*We proceed to the second article as follows:*

It seems that there cannot be a science of the divine realities that are matters of faith.

---

[14] See St. Thomas, *Contra gentiles* 3.19.
[15] St. Hilary, *De Trinitate* 2.10, CCL 62:48.14-16.

[1] See St. Thomas, *Sent.* 1, prol, q. un, a. 3, q. 2; *Summa theol.* 1.1.2.

*1.* For wisdom is different from science, and wisdom treats of the divine.[2] Therefore science does not.

*2.* As is said in the *Posterior Analytics*,[3] every science must presuppose knowledge of what its subject is. But, as Damascene says,[4] we can in no way know what God is. Therefore there can be no science of God.

*3.* It belongs to every science to study the parts and attributes of its subject.[5] But God, being a simple form, neither has parts into which he may be analyzed, nor can he be the subject of attributes.[6] Therefore there can be no science about God.

*4.* In every science reasoning comes before assent, for in the sciences demonstration is the cause of the assent to the objects of knowledge. But in objects of belief the opposite must be the case: as we have said,[7] the assent of faith precedes reasoning. Therefore there can be no science of divine realities, especially those accepted on faith.

*5.* Every science proceeds from self-evident principles which everyone accepts on hearing, or from principles that are trustworthy because of them. But the articles of faith, which are the first principles in matters of faith, are not of this sort. As has been said,[8] they are neither self-evident nor can they be resolved by demonstration to self-evident principles. Consequently there can be no science about the divine realities held on faith.

*6.* Faith is concerned with realities that are not evident,[9] whereas science is concerned with those that are evident, because science brings to light the objects with which it deals. Therefore there can be no science of the divine realities held on faith.

---

[2] See St. Augustine, *De Trinitate* 12.15.25, CCL 50:379.

[3] Aristotle, *Post. Anal.* 1.1 (71a11-13).

[4] St. John Damascene, *De fide orthodoxa* 1.2 and 4, ed. Buytaert, pp. 15.40-45 and 19.3-5, 20.33.

[5] See Aristotle, *Post. Anal.* 1.1.7, 10 (71a12, 75a39-b2, 76b11-16); St. Thomas, *In Peri herm.* 1, lect. 1, n. 3, ed. Leonine 1:8; *In Post. Anal.* 1, lect. 2, n. 2, ed. Leonine 1:142.

[6] See Boethius, *De Trinitate* 2, p. 10.29-30, 42-43 and p. 12.48-49.

[7] See above, a. 1, Reply, p. 38.

[8] See above, a. 1, Reply to 5, p. 39.

[9] See Hebrews 11:1.

7. Every science begins with understanding, because it is from the intellectual perception of principles that we arrive at the scientific knowledge of conclusions. But in matters of faith understanding does not come at the beginning but at the end, as is said in Isaiah 7:9[10]: "Unless you shall have believed, you will not understand." Hence there can be no science of the divine realities held by faith.

*On the contrary*, we have the words of Augustine[11]: "To this science I attribute only that whereby the most wholesome faith, which leads to true blessedness, is begotten, protected and strengthened." Therefore there is a science concerning matters of faith.

2. The same point is clear from the words of Wisdom 10:10: "Wisdom...gave him the science of the saints." This can only be understood to refer to that which distinguishes holy people from the wicked, namely the science of faith.

3. The Apostle, speaking of the knowledge possessed by the faithful in 1 Corinthians 8:7, says: "However, not all possess this science." From this the same conclusion follows.

*Reply:* The nature of science consists in this, that from things already known conclusions about other matters follow of necessity. Seeing that this is possible in the case of divine realities, clearly there can be a science about them. Now the knowledge of divine things can be interpreted in two ways. First, from our standpoint, and then they are knowable to us only through creatures, the knowledge of which we derive from the senses. Second, from the nature of divine realities themselves. In this way they are eminently knowable of themselves, and although we do not know them in their own way, this is how they are known by God and the blessed.

Accordingly there are two kinds of science concerning the divine. One follows our way of knowing, which uses the principles of sensible things in order to make the Godhead known. This is the way the philosophers handed down a science of the divine, calling the primary science "divine science." The other follows the mode of divine

---

[10] This is the reading of the Septuagint. The Vulgate reads: "If you will not believe, you shall not continue" (*Si non credideritis, non permanebitis*). See St. Jerome, *Commentaria in Esaiam prophetam* 3, PL 24:107A, CCL 73:99.84-88.

[11] St. Augustine, *De Trinitate* 14.1.3, CCL 50:424. The text of Aquinas mistakenly refers to book 12.

realities themselves, so that they are apprehended in themselves. We cannot perfectly possess this way of knowing in the present life, but there arises here and now in us a certain sharing in, and a likeness to, the divine knowledge, to the extent that through the faith implanted in us we firmly grasp the primary Truth itself for its own sake. And as God, by the very fact that he knows himself, knows all other things as well in his way, namely, by simple intuition without any reasoning process, so may we, from the things we accept by faith in our firm grasping of the primary Truth, come to know other things in our way, namely by drawing conclusions from principles. [12] Thus the truths we hold on faith are, as it were, our principles in this science, and the others become, as it were, conclusions. [13] From this it is evident that this science is nobler than the divine science taught by the philosophers, proceeding as it does from more sublime principles.

*Replies to Opposing Arguments:*

*Reply to 1.* Wisdom is not contrasted with science as though they were opposed to each other, but because wisdom adds an additional note to science. Wisdom, as the Philosopher says, [14] is the chief of all the sciences, because, being concerned with the highest principles, it directs all the other sciences. That is also why it is called the goddess of sciences in the beginning of the *Metaphysics*. [15] And this is even truer of the science that not only treats of the highest causes, but comes from them. [16] Now, since it belongs to the wise to direct others, so this most lofty science, which directs and puts order in the other sciences, is called wisdom, [17] just as in the "mechanical" arts they are called wise who draw up the plans for others, for example, architects. [18] The name "science" is left for the other less

---

[12] See St. Thomas, *Contra gentiles* 2.1.5.
[13] See St. Thomas, *Summa theol.* 1. 1. 7.
[14] Aristotle, *Nic. Ethics* 6.7 (1141a18-20).
[15] Aristotle, *Metaph.* 1.2 (983a6).
[16] See St. Thomas, *Summa theol.* 1.1.6.
[17] See St. Thomas, *Contra gentiles* 1.1.1.
[18] See Aristotle, *Metaph.* 1.1 (981a30-b3).

noble disciplines. In line with this, science is contrasted with wisdom as a property with a definition.[19]

*Reply to 2.* As was said above,[20] when causes are known through their effects knowledge of the effect takes the place of knowledge of the essence of the cause, and this is necessary in sciences that treat of realities knowable through themselves. Consequently, in order that we have a science of God, we need not first know what he is. Or we may reply that in divine science knowledge of what God is not takes the place of knowledge of what he is, for just as one thing is distinguished from others by what it is, so also by the knowledge of what it is not.

*Reply to 3.* By the parts of the subject in a science are to be understood not only subjective or integral parts,[21] but anything whatsoever, a knowledge of which is required for a knowledge of the subject, because a science is concerned with all matters of this sort only insofar as they are related to its subject. By attributes are meant whatever can be proved of anything, whether they are negative attributes or relations to other things. Many attributes of this sort can be proved of God, both from naturally known principles and from the principles of faith.

*Reply to 4.* In every science there are some items that function as principles and others that function as conclusions. The reasoning introduced in sciences precedes assent to the conclusions, but it follows assent to the principles because it flows from them. Now in divine science the articles of faith are like principles and not like conclusions. They are also defended against those who attack them, as the Philosopher[22] argues against those who deny principles.[23] Moreover they are clarified by certain analogies, just as principles

---

[19] The meaning of this enigmatic statement seems to be that wisdom is distinguished from science by something outside the definition of science, namely wisdom's office of directing the other sciences, as a property is distinguished from a definition as something outside the definition, for example, the capability of laughter is outside the definition "rational animal." See J. Owens, "A Note on Aquinas, *In Boeth. de Trin.*, 2, 2, ad 1ᵐ," *The New Scholasticism* 59 (1985), 102-108.

[20] See above, p. 24.

[21] For the meaning of these kinds of parts, see St. Thomas, *Summa theol.* 2-2. 48, a. un.

[22] Aristotle, *Metaph.* 4.4-6 (1005b35-1011b22).

[23] See St. Thomas, *Summa theol.* 1.1.8.

that are naturally known are made evident by induction but not proved by demonstrative reasoning.

*Reply to 5.* Even some of the sciences taught on the purely human level use principles that are not known to everyone, but they must be presupposed as established by higher sciences. Thus subalternate sciences employ principles that are presupposed and believed on the authority of higher sciences, and these principles are self-evident only to the higher sciences. It is in this way that the articles of faith, which are the principles of this science, are related to God's knowledge, because what is self-evident in the knowledge God has of himself is presupposed in our science,[24] and they are believed on the word of him who reveals them to us through his witnesses, in much the same way as a physician accepts the testimony of a scientist when he says that there are four elements.

*Reply to 6.* The evidence of a science is the result of the evidence of its principles, for a science does not make its principles evident, but because the principles are evident it renders its conclusions evident. In this way the science we are speaking about does not make matters of faith apparent, but by them it brings to light other things in the way we can be certain about the primary beings.[25]

*Reply to 7.* Understanding is always the primary source of every science, but it is not always its proximate source. Sometimes the proximate starting point of a science is belief, as is clear in the subalternated sciences. The proximate source of their conclusions is belief in truths presupposed as established by a higher science. Their primary source, however, is the knowledge of the higher scientist who, through his understanding, is certain about these matters of belief. Similarly the proximate starting point of this [divine] science is faith, but its primary source is the divine understanding, in which we put our faith. The purpose of our believing, however, is to arrive at an understanding of what we believe.[26] It is as if a scientist on a lower level acquired the science of a scientist on a higher level; he would then come to know and to understand what he formerly only believed.

---

[24] See ibid., 1.1.6, ad 1[m].
[25] See St. Thomas, *De veritate* 14.9, ad 3[m].
[26] See St. Thomas, *Sent.* 1, prol. q. un. a. 3, q. 3; *Quodlibet* 4, q. 9, a. 3.

### ARTICLE THREE

*Is It Permissible to Use Philosophical Reasoning and Authorities in the Science of Faith, Whose Object is God?*

*We proceed to the third article as follows:*

It seems that in matters of faith it is not permissible to use philosophical reasoning.

*1.* According to 1 Corinthians 1:17, "Christ did not send me to baptize but to preach the gospel, and not with eloquent wisdom," that is, "in the teaching of the philosophers," as the Gloss says.[1] And on the verse 1:20: "Where is the debater of this age?" the Gloss comments: "The debater is he who unravels the secrets of nature: such as these God does not accept as preachers."[2] Again, commenting on 2:4: "And my speech and my preaching was not in the persuasive words of human wisdom," the Gloss says: "Although my words were persuasive, they were not so because of human wisdom, like the words of pseudo-apostles."[3] From all this it seems that it is not permissible to use philosophical reasoning in matters of faith.

*2.* Commenting on Isaiah 15:1: "Ar is laid waste in a night," the Gloss say,[4] "Ar means the adversary, namely worldly knowledge, which is an enemy of God." Therefore we ought not to use worldly knowledge in matters that concern God.

*3.* Ambrose states[5]: "The mystery of faith is free from philosophical reasoning." Therefore, where it is a question of faith, it is not lawful to use the arguments and sayings of the philosophers.

*4.* Jerome[6] tells how in a vision he was scourged by divine judgment because he had read books of Cicero, how the bystanders prayed that he might be pardoned because of his youth, and then

---

[1] *Glossa ordinaria* 5, col. 201A. See Peter Lombard, *Glossa*, PL 191:1541B.
[2] *Glossa ordinaria* 6, col. 202D. See Peter Lombard, ibid., PL 191:1542D.
[3] Peter Lombard, ibid., PL 191:1548B. See *Glossa interlinearis* 6, col. 209-210.
[4] *Glossa ordinaria* 4, fol. 35rA.
[5] This statement is not from St. Ambrose but from Peter Lombard, *Sent.* 3, d. 22, c. 1, ed. Grottaferrata 2:136.8-9. See St. Ambrose, *De fide* 1.13.84, PL 16:570D.
[6] See St. Jerome, *Ep.* 22.30, CSEL 54:190.7-191.7.

how he would insist on being tortured if he ever again read books of the pagans. Calling to witness the name of God, he cried: "O Lord, if I ever possess and read secular books, I have denied you." Therefore if it is wrong to study and read them, much less is it permissible to use them in treatises about God.

5. Secular wisdom is often represented in Scripture by water, divine wisdom by wine. But in Isaiah 1:22, innkeepers are blamed for mixing water with wine. Consequently those teachers should be condemned who mingle philosophical doctrines with sacred teaching.

6. As Jerome says:[7] "We ought not to use the same language as heretics. But heretics use the teachings of philosophy in order to distort the faith, as is said in the Gloss on Proverbs 7:16 and Isaiah 15:5.[8] Therefore Catholics ought not to use them in their treatises.

7. Just as every science has its own principles,[9] so also does sacred doctrine, namely the articles of faith. But the other sciences proceed incorrectly if one science takes the principles of another; rather, each ought to proceed from its own principles, as the Philosopher teaches.[10] Therefore neither does sacred doctrine proceed correctly if anyone uses the teachings of philosophy.

8. If someone's teaching is rejected in a certain matter, his authority is weakened as a support for another. Thus Augustine says[11] that if we should grant any mistake in sacred Scripture, its authority as a support of faith will be destroyed. But sacred doctrine repudiates the teaching of the philosophers on many points because they are found to have made many mistakes. Therefore their authority is incapable of supporting anything.

*On the contrary*, the Apostle in Titus 1:12 uses a line of the poet Epimenides: "The Cretans are always liars, evil beasts, lazy gluttons"; in 1 Corinthians 15:33 he refers to the words of Menander: "Bad

---

[7] This statement has not been found in Jerome's gloss on Hosea. See *Glossa ordinaria* on Hosea 2:16; 4, fol. 336rA.

[8] See *Glossa ordinaria* on Proverbs 7:16; 3, col. 1634DE; and on Isaiah, 15:5; 4, fol. 35C.

[9] See Q. 6, a. 1, ed. Decker, p. 205.13-15, trans. Maurer, pp. 63-64; *In Post. Anal.* 1, lect. 41 and 43, ed. Leonine 1:306-307, n. 9-12 and 317, n. 13.

[10] Aristotle, *Post. Anal.* 1.7 (75a38-b20).

[11] St. Augustine, *Ep.* 28 *ad Hieronymum* 3.5 and 3.3, CSEL 34 (pt. 1), 111.8-13 and 108.5-10.

company ruins good morals''; and in Acts 17:28 to the Athenians he quotes the words of Aratus: "For we are indeed his (that is, God's) offspring.''[12] Consequently it is also permissible for other teachers of sacred Scripture to make use of philosophical arguments.

2. Jerome,[13] after mentioning several teachers of sacred Scripture like Basil, Gregory and certain others, adds, "All these so filled their books with the teachings and opinions of the philosophers that one does not know what to admire more in them, their secular learning or their knowledge of the Scriptures." They would not have acted like this had it been unlawful or useless.

3. Jerome wrote[14]: "If you love a captive woman, that is, worldly wisdom, and you are enthralled by her beauty, make her bald; do away with her alluring hair and verbal graces, along with her hard nails.[15] Wash her with the lye of which the prophet speaks,[16] and then reclining with her say[17]: 'Her left hand is under my head, and her right hand will embrace me.' Then will the captive woman bear you many children, and from a Moabitess she will become an Israelite woman to you.''[18] Therefore it is fruitful for one to use worldly wisdom.

4. Augustine states[19]: "I shall not be sluggish in seeking after the substance of God, whether through his Scripture or through his creature." Now the knowledge about creatures is set forth in philosophy. Therefore it is not unfitting for someone to use philosophical reasoning in sacred doctrine.

---

[12] Taken from St. Jerome, *Ep. 70 ad Magnum*, CSEL 54:701.9-11, 15-702.1. For Epimenides, see *The Pre-Socratic Philosohers*, ed. K. Freeman, p. 31. For Menander, see *Thais*, fragm. 197, ed. A. Koerte, *Menandri quae supersunt*, p. 2. For Aratus, see *Phaenomena*,v. 5, ed. E. Maass.

[13] St. Jerome, ibid., CSEL 54:706.14-707.3

[14] St. Jerome, *Ep. 56 ad Pammachium*, n. 8, CSEL 54:658.3-10. See also *Ep. 21 ad Damasum*, n. 13, CSEL 54:122.13-123.3 and 124.3-7; *Ep. 70 ad Magnum*, n. 2, CSEL 54:702.6-14.

[15] See Jeremiah 2:22.

[16] See Deut. 21:13.

[17] Cant. of Canticles 2:6.

[18] See Ruth 4:5, 10.

[19] St. Augustine, *De Trinitate* 2. prooem, 1, CCL 50:80.15-16.

5. Augustine writes[20]: "If those who are called philosophers have said things by chance that are true and in agreement with our faith, we must not only have no fear of them but appropriate them for our own use from those who are their unlawful possessors." And so the same conclusion follows.

6. Commenting on Daniel 1:8: "But Daniel resolved that he would not defile himself with the king's rich food," the Gloss says[21]: "If anyone who is ignorant of mathematics should write against the mathematicians, or knowing nothing of philosophy should attack the philosophers, who, even though himself a laughingstock, would not laugh?" But seeing that a teacher of sacred Scripture must at times oppose the philosophers, it is necessary for him to make use of philosophy.

*Reply*[22]: The gifts of grace are added to nature in such a way that they do not destroy it, but rather perfect it. So too the light of faith, which is imparted to us as a gift, does not do away with the light of natural reason given to us by God. And even though the natural light of the human mind is inadequate to make known what is revealed by faith, nevertheless what is divinely taught to us by faith cannot be contrary to what we are endowed with by nature. One or the other would have to be false, and since we have both of them from God, he would be the cause of our error, which is impossible. Rather, since what is imperfect bears a resemblance to what is perfect, what we know by natural reason has some likeness to what is taught to us by faith.

Now just as sacred doctrine is based on the light of faith, so philosophy is based on the natural light of reason. So it is impossible that the contents of philosophy should be contrary to the contents of faith, but they fall short of them. The former, however, bear certain likenesses to the latter and also contain certain preambles to them, just as nature itself is a preamble to grace. If anything, however, is found in the sayings of the philosophers contrary to faith, this is not

---

[20] St. Augustine, *De doctrina christiana* 2.40.60, CCL 32:73.1-4.

[21] *Glossa ordinaria*, 4, fol. 295rA. See St. Jerome, PL 25:497A.

[22] See St. Thomas, *Summa theol.* 1.1.8 and 2-2.1.5, ad 2 and 3; *Contra gentiles* 1.2 and 9; *Sent.*, 1, prol. a. 5; *Quodlibet* 4, q. 9, a. 3. *De rationibus fidei*, 2, ed. Leonine 40:B58.

philosophy but rather an abuse of philosophy arising from faulty reasoning. Therefore it is possible to refute an error of this sort by philosophical principles, either by showing that it is entirely impossible or that it is not necessary. For, as matters of faith cannot be demonstratively proved, so some assertions contrary to them cannot be demonstratively shown to be false; it can, however, be shown that they lack necessity.

Accordingly we can use philosophy in sacred doctrine in three ways.

First, in order to demonstrate the preambles of faith, which we must necessarily know in [the act of] faith. Such are the truths about God that are proved by natural reason, for example, that God exists, that he is one, and other truths of this sort about God or creatures proved in philosophy and presupposed by faith.

Second, by throwing light on the contents of faith by analogies, as Augustine[23] uses many analogies drawn from philosophical doctrines in order to elucidate the Trinity.

Third, in order to refute assertions contrary to the faith, either by showing them to be false or lacking in necessity.

Those, however, who use philosophy in sacred doctrine can err in two ways. In one way by making use of teachings that are contrary to the faith, which consequently do not belong to philosophy but are a corruption and abuse of it. Origen[24] was guilty of this. In another way by including the contents of faith within the bounds of philosophy, as would happen should somebody decide to believe nothing but what could be established by philosophy. On the contrary, philosophy should be brought within the bounds of faith, as the Apostle says in 2 Corinthians 10:5: "We...take every thought captive to obey Christ."

*Replies to Opposing Arguments:*

*Reply to 1.* All these statements show that the teaching of the philosophers is not to be used as though it held first place, in such a way that the truth of faith should be believed because of it. But this does not prevent teachers of sacred doctrine from being able to use it in a secondary role. Thus, commenting on the Apostle's words in the same letter (1:19): "I will destroy the wisdom of the wise,"

---

[23] St. Augustine, *De Trinitate* 9-12 and 14-15, CCL 50:292-380 and 421-533.

[24] Origen, see below, Q. 3, a. 4, p. 81.

the Gloss states[25]: "He says this, not because God can condemn the understanding of truth, but because he rejects the wisdom of those who rely on their own erudition." In order that all that belongs to faith should not be attributed to human power or wisdom, but to God alone, it was the will of God that the primitive apostolic preaching should have been marked by weakness and simplicity.[26] Nevertheless the power and secular wisdom that have come afterward show, by the triumph of the faith, that both as to power and wisdom the world is subject to God.

*Reply to 2.* Secular wisdom is said to be opposed to God in regard to its abuse, as when heretics misuse it, but not in regard to its truth.

*Reply to 3.* The mystery of faith is said to be free from philosophical reasoning because, as has been said, it is not confined within the bounds of philosophy.

*Reply to 4.* Jerome was so attached to pagan literature that in a way he held sacred Scripture in contempt, as he himself says:[27] "If when I came to myself I began to read the prophets, I was disgusted by their unpolished style." Nobody doubts that this deserves criticism.

*Reply to 5.* As the Master [Peter Lombard] says,[28] reasoning should not be based on figurative language. Dionysius also states that symbolic theology does not offer proofs, especially when it is interpreted by a writer who lacks authority. It can, however, be said that a mixture is not thought to have occurred when one of two items comes into the possession of the other, but when both of them are changed in their nature.[29] So those who use the works of the philosophers in sacred doctrine, by bringing them into the service of faith, do not mix water with wine, but rather change water into wine.

*Reply to 6.* Jerome speaks of the language created by heretics in accord with their errors. The philosophical disciplines are different;

---

[25] Peter Lombard, *Glossa*, PL 191:1543A.

[26] See St. Thomas, *De rationibus fidei* 7, ed. Leonine 40:B67.

[27] St. Jerome, *Ep. 22*, n. 30, CSEL 54:189.17.

[28] Peter Lombard, *Sent.* 3, d. 11, c. 2, n. 4, ed. Grottaferrata 2:80.3-4. See St. Thomas, *Sent.*, prol. q. un. a. 5c.

[29] For St. Thomas' doctrine of mixed bodies, see *De mixtione elementorum*, ed. Perrier, pp. 19-22; *Summa theol.* 1.76.4, ad 4; *Contra gentiles* 2.56.

only their misuse leads to error, and so they should not be avoided on this account.

*Reply to 7.* Interrelated sciences are such that one can use the principles of another. Sciences that come later employ the principles of prior sciences, whether the later be higher or lower in dignity. Thus metaphysics, which is the highest of the sciences, makes use of the conclusions established in the lower sciences. Similarly theology, to which all the other sciences are so to speak ancillary and propaedeutic in its coming into being, though they are of lesser dignity, can use the principles of all the other sciences.[30]

*Reply to 8.* Insofar as sacred doctrine uses philosophical teachings in its own interest, it does not welcome them because of the authority of their authors but on account of the reasonableness of what they say. What is well said it takes; the rest it rejects. But when it uses them to refute other writers, it does so because they are accepted as authorities by those who are refuted, for the witness of opponents carries greater weight.

ARTICLE FOUR

*Should Divine Realities be Veiled by Obscure and Novel Words?*[1]

*We proceed to the fourth article as follows:*

It seems that in the science of faith divine realities should not be veiled with obscure words.

*1.* For, as Proverbs 14:6 says, "Knowledge is easy for a man of understanding." Therefore it ought not to be presented in cryptic language.

---

[30] See St. Thomas, *Sent.*, prol. q. un. a. 1c, ed. Mandonnet 1:8; *Summa theol.* 1.1.5, sed contra and ad 2. The notion of philosophy as the handmaid of theology is found in Philo. See H. A. Wolfson, *Philo* 1:149-151.

[1] See St. Thomas, *Sent.* 1, d. 34, q. 3, a. 1, 2; *Summa theol.* 1.1.9, ad 2. The background of this question is the rule of secrecy practiced by the early Church, later called the "discipline of the secret" (*disciplina arcani*). See *The Oxford Dictionary of the Christian Church*, ed. F. L. Cross; 2nd ed. rev. F. L. Cross and E. A. Livingstone, p. 409. St. Thomas takes the occasion of Boethius' appeal to the discipline to insist that a teacher should adapt his words to the capacity of his hearers.

*2.* Ecclesiasticus 4:28 says, "Hide not your wisdom in her beauty," and Proverbs 11:26: "The people curse him who holds back grain." The Gloss understands by *grain* "preaching".[2] Therefore the words of sacred doctrine ought not to be hidden.

*3.* It is said in Matthew 10:27: "What I tell you in the dark, utter in the light." The Gloss interprets *in the dark* to mean "in mystery," and *utter in the light* to mean "openly."[3] So the mysteries of faith ought rather to be disclosed than hidden by difficult language.

*4.* Teachers of the faith have obligations to the learned and to the unlearned, as is clear from Romans 1:14. Therefore they ought to talk in such a way that they can be understood by both the great and the simple, that is, without obscure language.

*5.* Wisdom 7:13 says: "I learned without guile and impart without grudging." But the one who hides wisdom does not impart it. Therefore he seems to be guilty of jealousy.

*6.* Augustine states[4]: "The interpreters of sacred Scripture should not speak as though they were proposing themselves for interpretation, but in all their words their first and greatest endeavor should be to make themselves understood as much as possible by such clearness of style that the person who does not understand is very stupid."

*On the contrary,* Matthew 7:6 says: "Do not give dogs what is holy; and do not throw your pearls before swine." The Gloss comments on this: "What is hidden is more eagerly sought after; what is concealed appears more worthy of reverence; what is searched for longer is more dearly prized."[5] Therefore, since the sacred teachings should be regarded with the utmost reverence, it seems that they ought not to be made accessible to the public, but taught in obscure language.

2. Dionysius says: "You should not commit to everyone all the holy doctrines of the sublime episcopal order, but only to the godlike teachers of sacred things of the same rank as yourself." In other words, teach the divine praises, which include all the sacred writings, only to your peers. But if they were written in clear language, they

---

[2] *Glossa ordinaria* 3, col. 1651-1652; *Glossa interlinearis,* lin. 10(a).
[3] *Glossa ordinaria* 5, fol. 37v, *Glossa interlinearis,* lin. o.
[4] St. Augustine, *De doctrina christiana* 4.8.22, CCL 32:131.11-132.15.
[5] *Glossa ordinaria* 5, fol. 28rB.

would be obvious to all. So the mysteries of faith should be concealed in obscure language.

3. Luke 8:10 is to the point. He says: "To you," that is, to the perfect, "it has been given to know the secrets of the kingdom of God," that is, an understanding of the Scriptures, as is clear from the Gloss, "but for others they are in parables"[6]. So there are some things that should be hidden by obscure language.

*Reply*: A teacher should so measure his words that they help rather than hinder his hearer. Now there are some things which can harm nobody when they are heard, for example, the truths everyone is bound to know. These should not be concealed but taught openly to everyone. There are other matters, however, that would be harmful to those hearing them if they were openly presented. This can happen in two ways. First, if the secrets of faith were revealed to unbelievers who detest the faith, for they would receive them with ridicule. Hence the Lord says in Matthew 7:6: "Do not give dogs what is holy," and Dionysius states[7]: "Concealing the holy truths, guard them from the profane crowd as something unchanging." Second, when abstruse doctrines are taught to the uneducated they take an occasion of error from what they do not fully understand. Thus the Apostle says in 1 Corinthians 3:1-2: "But I, brethren, could not address you as spiritual men, but as babes in Christ. I fed you with milk, not solid food." Commenting on Exodus 21:33: "When someone leaves a pit open," etc., Gregory says[8]: "Anyone who now perceives the depths in the sacred words, should hide in silence their sublime meaning when in the presence of those who do not understand them, so that he will not hurt by interior scandal an immature believer or an unbeliever who might become a believer." These matters, therefore, ought to be concealed from those to whom they might do harm.

In speaking, however, it is possible to discriminate. Certain things can be explained to the wise in private which we should keep silent about in public. Thus Augustine says[9]: "There are some passages

---

[6] Ibid., fol. 146v; *Glossa interlinearis*. lin. a.

[7] Pseudo-Dionysius, *De caelesti hierarchia* 2.5, PG 3:145C.

[8] St. Gregory, *Moralia* 17.26.38, CCL 143A:872. See *Glossa ordinaria* 1, col. 697B.

[9] St. Augustine, *De doctrina christiana* 9.23, CCL 32:132.1-5.

which are not understood in their proper force or are understood with difficulty, no matter how great, how comprehensive, or how clear the eloquence with which they are handled by the speaker. These should be spoken to a public audience only rarely, if there is some urgent reason, or never at all." In writing, however, this distinction does not hold because a written book can fall into the hands of anybody. Therefore these matters should be concealed with obscure language, so that they will benefit the wise who understand them and be hidden from the uneducated who are unable to grasp them. This puts a burden on no one, for those who understand will go on reading them and those who do not are not obliged to read them at all. So Augustine continues:[10] "In books that are written in such a style that, when understood, they themselves so to speak grip the reader's attention, but, when not understood, give no trouble to those who do not care to read them, we must not neglect the duty of bringing truths, though very hard to understand, to the knowledge of others."

*Replies to Opposing Arguments*:

*Reply to 1.*   This text is not to the point. It does not mean that the teaching of the wise is easy in the active sense, that is, that they teach easily, but rather in the passive sense, that they are easily taught. This is clear from the Gloss.[11]

*Reply to 2.*   These texts refer to one who conceals what he ought to reveal. Thus Ecclesiasticus 4:28 says immediately before: "Do not refrain from speaking in the time of salvation." The fact is not denied that what should be hidden ought to be concealed in obscure language.

*Reply to 3.*   The teaching of Christ should be publicly and openly preached, so that it is clear to everyone what is good for him to know, but not that what is not good for him to know be made public.

*Reply to 4.*   The obligation of the teachers of sacred Scripture to the wise and the unwise does not extend to their proposing the same things to both, but to telling each what is appropriate to them.

---

[10] Ibid.
[11] *Glossa ordinaria* 3, col. 1662D.

*Reply to 5.* It is not from jealousy that difficult truths are hidden from the masses, but rather, as has been said,[12] from due discretion.

*Reply to 6.* Augustine is referring to interpreters who speak to the people, not to those who teach something in writing. This is clear from his next words.[13]

---

[12] See above, Reply, pp. 53-54.

[13] The words that follow are: "...or the reason why what we say is not understood, or is understood rather slowly, lies not in our manner of speaking, but in the difficulty and subtlety of the matters which we are trying to explain and make clear."

# BOETHIUS

## DE TRINITATE, CHAPTER 1

There are many who claim as theirs the piety of the Christian religion, but that faith is most valid and only valid which, both because of the universal nature of its rules, by which we can recognize this religion's authority, and because its worship has spread almost to the ends of the earth, is called catholic or universal.

The belief of this religion regarding the unity of the Trinity is as follows: the Father, they say, is God, the Son is God, and the Holy Spirit is God. Therefore the Father, Son and Holy Spirit are one God, not three gods. The reason for this unity is absence of difference. Difference is inevitable for those who add to or take away from the unity, as for example the Arians, who, by positing degrees of merit in the Trinity diversify it, break it up and reduce it to a plurality. For the source of plurality is otherness; apart from otherness plurality is unintelligible. In fact, the diversity of three or more things lies in genus, species or number. Things are said to be diverse in as many ways as they are said to be the same. Now they are called the same in three ways: in genus, for example, a man and a horse, because they are in the same genus of animal; or in species, for example, Cato and Cicero, because they are in the same species of man; or in number, for example, Tully and Cicero, because he is one in number. Therefore difference is also expressed by genus, species or number. Now numerical difference is caused by diversity of accidents; three men differ neither in genus nor species but by their accidents, for if we mentally remove from them all [other] accidents, still each occupies a different place, which we cannot possibly conceive to be the same, for two bodies cannot occupy the same place, and place is an accident. So they are many in number because they are made many by their accidents.

## St. Thomas' Literal Commentary

Having concluded his preface, Boethius here begins his treatise on
the Trinity of persons and the unity of the divine essence. The book
is divided into two parts. In the first he deals with topics relating to
the unity of the divine essence, in opposition to the Arians. In the
second, beginning with the words "Let this be enough for the present,"[1]
he treats of subjects concerning the Trinity of persons, against
Sabellius.[2]

The first part has two sections. In the first he sets forth the doctrine
of the Catholic faith regarding the unity of the divine essence. In the
second, at the words, "We will now begin a careful consideration,"[3]
he inquires into the truth of the doctrine. The first section in turn
has two parts. In the first he describes a characteristic of the faith
whose teaching he intends to investigate. In the second, at the words
"The belief of this religion," he explains the doctrine of the faith
he has described regarding the present topic. He describes it in two
ways: by comparison with heresies, which it excels, and by its own
title, for it is called catholic or universal.

He says then, "There are many," that is, various heretical sects,
"who claim as theirs," that is, unlawfully ascribe to themselves "the
piety of the Christian religion," that is, what is due to this religion,
for example, that everyone is subject to it, as we read in 1 John 5:4:
"This is the victory that overcomes the world, our faith." Or [they
usurp] the "piety" that the Christian religion shows to God by
believing what has been divinely taught. Then he continues: "but
that faith is most valid and exclusively valid," etc. He adds these
two expressions to make a distinction between a matter of truth and
a matter of opinion. As far as true doctrine is concerned, heretics
are not Christians because they fall away from Christ's teachings,
and in this respect the Catholic faith alone is valid. But if we regard
only outward appearance and human judgments, heretics are given
the name "Christian," for at least verbally they confess the name
of Christ, and in this respect the Catholic faith is not the only one

---

[1] Boethius, *De Trinitate* 3, ed. Stewart, Rand and Tester, p. 17.41.
[2] For the errors of Arius and Sabellius, see St. Thomas, *Contra gentiles* 4.5-9.
[3] Boethius, *De Trinitate* 2, p. 9.1.

that is valid, but it is most valid, for it is more generally and widely accepted. So he adds, which "is called catholic" in Greek "or universal" in Latin; for catholic in Greek means universal in Latin.

He gives two reasons for this title, saying "both because of the universal nature of its rules," for the precepts of the Catholic faith are not meant to be observed by one race alone but by everyone. In this respect it differs especially from the Law of Moses, which laid down precepts for only one people. So too individual heresies prescribe rules suited only to their members, while the Catholic faith, having the care of all, gives rules adapted to everyone: not only to the unmarried, like the Manichees,[4] but also to the married; not only to the innocent, like the Novatians,[5] but to penitents as well, to whom they deny salvation. So he adds "by which," that is, its universal laws, "we can recognize this religion's authority," in virtue of which all ought to be subject to it. Or they are called universal laws because they contain nothing false or evil in any article or in any case. He then adds another reason [for the title "universal"], saying "and because its worship has spread almost to the ends of the earth." This is clear in Psalm 18:5: "Yet their voice goes out through all the earth, and their words to the ends of the world."

Then when Boethius says, "The belief of this religion regarding the unity of the Trinity," etc., he states the teaching of the Catholic faith regarding the question raised above. In this connection he makes three points. First, he presents the teaching of the Catholic faith concerning the unity of the Trinity. Second, he gives the reason for the doctrine, when he says, "The reason for this unity," etc. Third, he shows the fittingness of this reason at the words "For the source of plurality," etc. He puts the belief of the Catholic faith in the form of an argument, for faith is "the evidence" (*argumentum*) "of things that do not appear" (Hebrews 11:1). In this argument he concludes from the fact that the Godhead is attributed exactly in the same way to each of the persons, that the name "God" is said of all three not in the plural but in the singular.

---

[4] See St. Thomas, *Contra gentiles* 3.126.6. The allusion is to the Albigensians or Cathari, who in this respect followed the Manichees.

[5] See St. Thomas, *Contra gentiles* 4.71.9.

Next he gives the reason for this belief. First, he states the reason. Second, he explains it by its contrary, when he says "Difference is inevitable," etc. He says: "The reason for this unity," that is, [the basis] of the whole argument, "is absence of difference," namely of Godhead in the three persons, which the Catholic faith confesses. For it is because undifferentiated divinity is ascribed indifferently to the three persons that the above conclusion follows from the premises. He then explains this reason by its contrary, saying "Difference," that is, within the Godhead, "is inevitable for those who add to or take away," that is, who claim that one person is superior or inferior to another, like the Arians, who hold that the Father is greater than the Son. So he adds: "who," that is, the Arians, "by positing degrees of merit," that is, of eminence, "in the Trinity diversify it" when they subordinate the Son to the Father and the Holy Spirit to both, "break it up," that is, they force the Godhead into different beings by parceling it out in them, "and reduce it to a plurality", for plurality follows upon division.[6] Catholics, on the contrary, who believe in the equality of the persons, profess their absence of difference and consequently their unity.

Then when he says, "For the source of plurality is otherness," he shows the fittingness of this reasoning. This is divided into two parts. In the first he points out the necessity involved in the above reasoning. In the second he proves a proposition presupposed in his proof, when he says, "In fact, the diversity of all[7] things," etc. In connection with the first he makes two points. First, that otherness (alteritas) is the source of plurality, understanding by otherness the difference that makes one thing other (alterum) than something else. He preferred to say "otherness" (alteritatem) rather than "difference" (alietatem) because plurality results not only from substantial differences, which make one thing other than another thing, but also from accidental differences, which make one thing different from something else.[8] Otherness is a consequence of difference, but not

---

[6] See below, Q. 4, a. 1, p. 89.

[7] St. Thomas' text has *Omnium* in place of the Boethian *Trium*.

[8] *Alteritas* is the otherness resulting particularly from accidental differences, for example, from red and green. In a broad sense it means the otherness resulting from both accidental and substantial differences. See below, Q. 4, a. 1, reply to 5, p. 92. *Alietas* is dissimilarity or difference in substance or subject, for example, between man and dog.

vice versa. This gives us the basis of the argument of the Arians. For, if otherness is the source of plurality, and the effect follows upon the cause, it follows that those who introduce otherness into the deity, admitting of degrees of perfection, posit a plurality in it.

Second, he states that otherness is the proper principle of plurality because without it plurality is unintelligible. From this we can grasp the reason for the Catholic doctrine of the divine unity. If the proper principle is taken away, so too is the effect. Consequently, if there is no otherness of Godhead in the three persons, there will be no plurality in it, but only unity.

Then when he says, "In fact, the diversity of all things," etc.[9] he proves the proposition he had presupposed, namely that otherness is the proper principle of plurality. The argument goes as follows: In all things differing in genus, species or number, there is some otherness or difference causing the diversity. But all multiple things, whether they be three or any number you wish, are different either in genus, species or number. Therefore some kind of otherness is the ground of all multiple things. In connection with this argument he does three things. First, he states the minor premise, second its proof, beginning "Things are said to be diverse," etc. The proof goes as follows: Things are said to be diverse in as many ways as they are said to be the same. Now they are called the same in three ways: in genus, species and number. Hence they are called diverse in the same three ways. He bases the first proposition on the statement in the Topics,[10] that as often as we refer to one of two opposites, we also refer to the other; and also on the words of the Metaphysics,[11] that the same and different are opposites. The second proposition he clarifies by examples, and he bases it on the Topics.[12] Third, he proves the major premise, touching on a matter that could be in doubt, saying "Now numerical difference," etc. It is clear from the word itself that some otherness is the source of the diversity of things different in genus or species. For things are different in genus because they belong to another genus, and they are different in species because

[9] See above, note 7.
[10] Aristotle, Topics 1.15 (106b13-15, 21-23 and 107a33-35).
[11] Aristotle, Metaph. 10.3 (1054b22); see also 5.9 (1018a12).
[12] See note 10 above.

they belong to another species. But it is not evident from the word itself that some otherness is the source of the difference and plurality of things said to be numerically different. Rather, from the word itself the converse might seem to be the case, that plurality in number is the source of diversity, because from the word itself things are said to be different in number just as they are said to be different in genus or species. And therefore in order to prove the major premise of his syllogism he shows that there is some kind of otherness or variety that produces even the difference by which some things are said to differ in number. The proof is that in three men who are in the same genus and species there are different accidental characteristics, just as a man and an ox are in different species, and a man and a stone are in different genera. Consequently, just as a man and an ox are unlike in species, so two men are unlike in accidental characteristics.

Someone might object that a difference in accidental traits does not cause a plurality in number, because if accidents are taken away— either actually, as in the case of separable accidents, or by the mind or in thought, as in the case of inseparable accidents—the subjects still continue to exist, because an accident can be present or absent without the destruction of its subject. He meets this objection by pointing out that, although all accidents can be removed, at least mentally, nevertheless there is one accidental difference that can in no way—not even mentally—be separated from different individuals, namely difference of place. Two bodies cannot occupy the same place whether in fact or in fiction, for this is neither intelligible nor imaginable. So he concludes: "So they," that is, men, "are many in number because they are many," that is, different, "by their accidents." With this he brings to a close the teaching of this part of his treatise.

# QUESTION THREE

# ON TOPICS RELATING TO THE PRAISE OF FAITH

There are two questions here. The first concerns topics relating to the praise of faith; the second has to do with factors relating to the cause of plurality.

With regard to the first, there are four points of inquiry:

1. Is faith necessary for the human race?
2. How faith is related to religion.
3. Is the true faith fittingly called catholic or universal?
4. Does the true faith affirm that the Father, the Son and the Holy Spirit are each God, and that the three are one God without differing by being unequal?

ARTICLE ONE

*Is Faith Necessary for the Human Race?*[1]

*We proceed to the first article as follows:*

It seems that it was not necessary for the human race to have faith.

*1.* For, as Ecclesiastes says (7:1), "What need is there for a person to seek what is above him?" as though to say, no need whatsoever. Now the teachings of faith are above us, transcending our reason. If this were not so, reason, which produces science, would have been adequate for a knowledge of these matters and there would have been no need of faith. Therefore there was no necessity for us, in addition, to have been taught the doctrines of faith.

---

[1] See St. Thomas, *Sent.* 3, d. 24, a. 3, q. 1; *De veritate* 14.10; *Contra gentiles* 1.4-5 and 4.1; *Summa theol.* 1.1.1 and 2-2.2.3-4.

*2.* God created human nature in a perfect state; as Deuteronomy says (32:4), "The works of God are perfect." Now mankind cannot come to a knowledge of the things of faith from what was given to the human mind at its creation; otherwise they could be known through science, which results from conclusions being resolved into naturally known principles. Therefore, since something is called perfect to which nothing due to it is lacking, as the *Metaphysics* says,[2] it seems that mankind does not need faith.

*3.* To reach his goal a wise man chooses the road that is easiest and freest from obstructions. But it seems most difficult and very dangerous for us to believe what lies beyond reason, for many fall from the state of salvation because they do not believe. Therefore it seems that God, who is most wise, ought not to have provided us with the road of faith to salvation.

*4.* An easy way to make a mistake is to assent uncritically to cognitive matters. But we do not have the capacity to make judgments about the things we accept on faith because our natural power of judgment does not extend to them, for they are beyond reason. So this opens an easy road to error. Consequently it seems to be harmful rather than useful to us to be directed to God by faith.

*5.* As Dionysius says,[3] it is wrong for one to go against reason. But the person who clings to faith flees from reason and thereby also becomes accustomed to despise reason. So it seems that this path is harmful to us.

*On the contrary,* it is said in Hebrews 11:6: "Without faith it is impossible to please God." Now it is most fitting that we please God, without whom we can do or have nothing good. So faith is most necessary for humankind.

2. Knowing the truth is most necessary for us, because happiness is joy in the known truth, as Augustine says.[4] But, as Dionysius remarks,[5] "Faith establishes believers in the truth and the truth in them." So faith is most necessary for humankind.

---

[2] Aristotle, *Metaph.* 5.16 (1021b12).

[3] Pseudo-Dionysius, *De divinis nominibus* 4.32. PG 3:733A. See St. Thomas, *Summa theol.* 1-2.18.5 and 71.2.

[4] St. Augustine, *Confessions* 10.23.33. CCL 27:173.10.

[5] Pseudo-Dionysius, *De divinis nominibus* 7.4. PG 3:871C.

3. What is needed to preserve human society is most necessary for the human race, because "man is by nature a political animal," as is said in the *Ethics*.[6] Now society cannot be preserved without faith, for one person must believe another in making promises and giving witness and the like, which are necessary in order that we might live together.[7] Therefore faith is very necessary for the human race.

*Reply*: Faith[8] has something in common with opinion and also with science and understanding; so Hugh of St. Victor places it between science and opinion.[9] With science and understanding it has in common unerring and firm assent.[10] In this respect it differs from opinion, which accepts one of two contraries but fears the other might be correct, and also from doubt, which hesitates between two contraries. With opinion it shares the fact that it has to do with matters that are not clear to the mind, in which respect it differs from science and understanding. Now, as the *Metaphysics* says[11], there can be two reasons why something is not evident to human knowledge: because of something wanting on the part of the knowable objects themselves, and because of some deficiency on the part of our mind. Examples of something wanting on the part of objects are individual and contingent things that are remote from our senses, for example, our actions, words and thoughts, which are such that they can be known to one person and unknown to another.[12] And because in human society one person must make use of another just as he does himself in matters in which he is not self-sufficient, he must take his stand on what another knows and is unknown to himself, just as he does on what he himself knows. As a consequence, faith is necessary in human society, one person believing what another

    [6] Aristotle, *Nic. Ethics* 9.9 (1169b18) and 1.5 (1097b11). The text of St. Thomas refers to book 8. See *Politics* 1.2, (1253a2) and 3.6 (1278b19).

    [7] See St. Thomas, *Expos. super symbolum apost.*, ed. Spiazzi, n. 866, p. 193.

    [8] On the notion of faith, see St. Thomas, *Sent.* 3, d. 23, q. 2, a. 1 and 2; *De veritate* 14.1; *Summa theol.* 2-2.2.1 and 4.1; *In Hebr.* 11, lect. 1, ed. Marietti, nn. 551-560, 2:457-459.

    [9] Hugh of St. Victor, *De sacramentis christianae fidei* 10.2, PL 176:330C.

    [10] See St. Augustine, *De praedestinatione sanctorum* 2.5, PL 44:963.

    [11] Aristotle, *Metaph.* 2.1 (993b7-9).

    [12] See St. Thomas, *Summa theol.* 2-2.171.3.

says. As Cicero remarks,[13] this is the basis of justice. That is why there is no lie without moral fault,[14] for every lie does some harm to this so essential faith.

Owing to a deficiency on our part, divine and necessary realities, which are most knowable by nature, are not apparent to us. We are not adapted to examine them from the outset, because we have to arrive at what is more knowable and prior by nature beginning with what is less knowable and posterior by nature. But what we first know is known on the strength of what we eventually come to know; so from the very beginning we must have some knowledge of those things which are more knowable in themselves, and this is possible only by faith. The sequence of the sciences makes this clear, for the science that concerns the highest causes, namely metaphysics,[15] comes last in human knowledge, and yet the sciences that precede it must presuppose certain truths that are more fully elucidated in that science.[16] As a result, every science has presuppositions which the learner must believe.[17] Consequently, since the goal of human life is perfect happiness, which consists in the full knowledge of divine realities, the direction of human life toward perfect happiness from the very beginning requires faith in the divine, the complete knowledge of which we look forward to in our final state of perfection.[18]

Even in the present life it is possible for us to arrive by reasoning at a full knowledge of some divine things. But even though we can have knowledge of them, and some persons actually achieve it, faith is still necessary, and this for five reasons given by Rabbi Moses.[19]

First, owing to the depth and subtlety of the subject matter, which conceals the divine from human minds. Consequently, lest the human race be without any knowledge of things divine, provision was made

---

[13] Cicero, De officiis 1.7.23.
[14] See St. Thomas, Summa theol. 2-2.110.3.
[15] See above, Q. 2, a. 2, Reply to 1, p. 42.
[16] See Q. 5, a. 1, Reply to 9 and Q. 6, a. 1, ad tert. quaest., ed. Decker, pp. 172.3-20 and 210-212, trans. Maurer, pp. 23-24 and 70-73.
[17] See Aristotle, De sophisticis elenchis 2 (165b3).
[18] See St. Thomas, De veritate 14.10; Contra gentiles 3.152.4; Summa theol. 2-2.2.3.
[19] Moses Maimonides, Guide of the Perplexed 1. 33. See St. Thomas, Sent. 3, d. 24, q. 1, a. 3; De veritate 14.10; Contra gentiles 1.4; Summa theol. 1.1.1 and 2-2.2.4.

that it might know them at least by faith. As Ecclesiastes says (7:25). "It is a great depth, and who shall find it out?" The second reason is the initial weakness of the human mind, which reaches its perfection only at the end. So, in order that it should at no time lack a knowledge of God, it needs faith, through which it may accept divine things from the very beginning. Third, because of the many preliminary items of knowledge that are needed to reach a knowledge of God by human reasoning. Indeed a knowledge of almost all the sciences is required for this, since the purpose of all of them is the knowledge of God. And yet, very few persons reach these preliminaries. So, in order that a large portion of the human race will not be left without a knowledge of God, he has provided the way of faith for them. Fourth, because many persons by their physical dispositions are unsuited to reach perfection of mind by the use of reason, the way of faith has been provided so that these also may not be wanting in divine knowledge. Fifth, because of the many occupations in which we must be engaged. This makes it impossible for everyone to acquire the necessary knowledge about God by way of reasoning. For this reason the way of faith has been provided, and here we are concerned with those matters which are known by some people but are proposed to others for belief.

There are, however, some aspects of the divinity that human reason is utterly incapable of knowing fully; we await their clear knowledge in the life to come, where our happiness will be complete. An example is the unity and trinity of the one God. We shall be advanced to this knowledge not by anything due to our nature but only by divine grace. So, even for this perfect knowledge certain presuppositions must be offered at the beginning for our belief, and from these we are led to the full knowledge of the things we believe from the beginning. As has been said, [20] the same thing happens in the other sciences. Thus it is said in Isaiah (7:9), according to another version: "Unless you shall have believed you will not understand". [21] Presuppositions of this sort are objects of belief for everyone; in this life no one knows or understands them.

[20] See above, Q. 2, a. 2, Reply to 5, p. 44.
[21] See above, ibid., p. 41, n. 10.

*Replies to Opposing Arguments:*

*Reply to 1.* Though the teachings of faith are above us from the standpoint of our natural powers, they are not above us as elevated by the divine light. So it is not necessary for us to seek out these matters by our own power, but we must know them by divine revelation.

*Reply to 2.* In the original creation of the world God made us perfect with the perfection of nature, which consists in our having everything due to our nature. But over and above what is due to our nature there were later added to the human race certain perfections that were solely owing to divine grace. Among these is faith, which is a "gift of God," as is clear from Ephesians 2:8.

*Reply to 3.* All who strive for perfect happiness must know in what and how they ought to seek it. Now this could not be done more easily than by faith, because rational inquiry cannot reach these matters without a previous knowledge of many items which are not easy to know. Nor could it be done with little danger, for, owing to the weakness of our mind, human inquiry is prone to error. This is evident from the philosophers themselves, who in their rational search for the goal of human life and the means to attain it fell into many shameful errors.[22] They disagreed with each other so much that scarcely two or three were of the same opinion in every respect about these matters. Yet we see that through faith even a great number of nations are united in a common way of thinking.

*Reply to 4.* Whenever assent is in any way given to accepted positions there must be something that disposes the mind to the assent. Thus the light with which we are naturally endowed causes assent to self-evident first principles, and the truth of the principles themselves moves us to assent to the conclusions known through them, and probabilities incline us to assent to our opinions. If these probabilities were somewhat stronger they would cause us to believe, for faith is said to be opinion supported by reasons.[23] Now that which inclines us to assent to understood principles or known conclusions is an adequate motive force; it even compels assent and it suffices for a judgment about that to which assent is given. But what inclines us to form an opinion in any way whatsoever—even strongly—is

---

[22] See St. Thomas, *Expos. super symbolum apost.*, ed. Spiazzi, n. 862, p. 193.
[23] See St. Thomas, *Sent.*, 1, prol. q. un., a. 3, q. 3, sol. 3.

not a sufficient motive force. So it does not compel assent, nor does it enable us to form a perfect judgment about that to which we give assent.

So also in the faith by which we believe in God there is not only the accepting of the object of assent, but something moving us to the assent. This is a kind of light—the habit of faith—divinely imparted to the human mind. It is more capable of causing assent than any demonstration. Though a demonstration never leads to a false conclusion, we often mistakenly think something is a demonstration that is not. It is also more capable than the natural light itself by which we assent to principles, because that light is often hindered by bodily ailments, as is clear in the insane, but the light of faith, which is, as it were, a faint stamp of the First Truth in our mind,[24] cannot fail, any more than God can be deceived or lie. Thus this light is an adequate means of making judgments. The habit of faith, however, does not move us by way of the intellect, but rather by way of the will. As a consequence it does not make us see what we believe, nor does it force our assent, but it causes us to assent to it voluntarily.[25]

It is clear, then, that faith comes from God in two ways: by way of an interior light that leads to assent, and by way of the realities that are proposed from without and that had as their source divine revelation.[26] These are related to the knowledge of faith as the things perceived by the sense are related to the knowledge of principles, for both make our knowledge certain. So just as the knowledge of principles is taken from the senses, and yet the light by which principles are known is inborn, so "faith comes from hearing,"[27] and nevertheless the habit of faith is infused.

*Reply to 5.* Living according to reason is our good insofar as we are human. Living apart from reason in one sense can be taken as a defect, as in the case of those who live sensually; and this is an evil for us. In another sense it can mean an excess, as when a person is led by divine grace to what is above reason. In the latter

---

[24] See above, Q. 2, a. 2, p. 42.
[25] See St. Thomas, *Contra gentiles* 3.40.3.
[26] See St. Thomas, *Summa theol.* 2-2.6.1.
[27] Romans 10:17.

sense living apart from reason is not an evil for us but a good that is above us. Knowledge of the truths of faith is of this sort, though faith itself is not entirely apart from reason, for natural reason maintains that we should assent to the words of God.

ARTICLE TWO

## How Faith Is Related to Religion

*We proceed to the second article as follows:*

It seems that faith should not be distinguished from religion.

*1.* For, as Augustine says,[1] God should be worshiped by faith, hope and love. Now the worship of God is an act of religion, as is clear from the definition of Cicero[2], who says that "religion is that which offers worship and rites to a certain higher nature, which is called divine." Therefore faith is a part of religion.

*2.* Augustine states[3] that true religion is that "by which the one God is honored and known with the purest piety." But to know God is a matter of faith. Therefore faith is contained under religion.

*3.* Offering sacrifice to God is an act of religion. Now this belongs to faith, because, as Augustine says,[4] "True sacrifice is every work done so that we may adhere to God in holy fellowship." Now we first adhere to God through faith. So faith especially belongs to religion.

*4.* In John 4:24 it is said: "God is spirit, and those who worship him must worship in spirit and truth." It follows that we adore God more properly when we submit our mind to him than when we incline our body to him. But we submit our mind to him through faith when the mind completely submits to assent to the words of God. So faith is most closely associated with religion.

*5.* Every virtue that has God for its object is a theological virtue.[5] Now religion has God for its object, for to God alone does it offer

[1] St. Augustine, *Enchiridion* 1.3, CCL 46:49.21.
[2] Cicero, *De inventione* 2.53.161.
[3] St. Augustine, *De vera religione* 1.1, CCL 32:187.2-3.
[4] St. Augustine, *De civitate Dei* 10.6, CCL 47:278.1-2.
[5] See St. Thomas, *Summa theol.* 1-2.62.1 and 2.

fitting adoration. Therefore it is a theological virtue. But it seems to be associated with faith more than with any of the other virtues, since only those are said to be outside the Christian religion who are outside the faith. Therefore religion seems to be identical with faith.

*On the contrary*, Cicero[6] makes religion a part of justice, which is a cardinal virtue. Consequently, since faith is a theological virtue, religion will belong to a different genus than faith.

2. Religion also consists in activity regarding our neighbor, as is clear in James 1:27: "Religion that is pure and undefiled before God and the Father is this: to visit orphans and widows in their affliction, and to keep oneself unstained from the world." But all acts of faith are related to God.[7] Therefore religion is entirely distinct from faith.

3. Those are commonly called religious who are bound by special vows. But they are not the only ones called the faithful. Consequently the faithful and religious are not identical, and so neither are faith and religion.

*Reply*:  Augustine[8] makes it clear that *theosebia* (which means the worship of God), religion, piety and adoration are taken to be connected with the same thing, that is, devotion to God. Now the devotion (*cultus*) given to anything seems to be nothing more than an appropriate act performed in its regard. Thus we are said to be devoted (*colere*) in various ways to fields, parents, country and the like, because different acts are fitting for different things. But God is not given devotion in such a way that our action would do him some good or help him, as in the cases mentioned above, but only because we submit ourselves to him and show ourselves to be his subjects. Therefore divine worship (*cultus divinus*) is perfectly expressed by the word *theosebia*. But religion implies a kind of binding, in the sense that a person in a way obliges himself to this worship. Thus, as Augustine says,[9] the word "religion" is thought to be derived from *religare* (to bind back), or also from *reeligere* (to choose again),

---

[6] Cicero, *De inventione* 2.22.65.

[7] See St. Thomas, *Summa theol.* 2-2.81.1.

[8] St. Augustine, *De civitate Dei* 10.1, CCL 47:272.36-274.100.

[9] St. Augustine, *De vera religione* 55.113, CCL 32: 259.122. For St. Thomas' notion of religion, see *Contra gentiles* 3.119; *Summa theol.* 2-2.81.1.

as he says in the *City of God*.[10] For by one's own choice a person is bound to do something. Now we must "choose again" him whom "we have lost by our neglect," as he says in the same book.[11] As a result, those who by certain vows dedicate their whole life and themselves to allegiance to God are called religious.

Piety, however, has to do with the soul of the worshiper, who pledges his service not by pretence or out of love of gain. And because a kind of divine reverence is due to those above us, even the favors we show to the unfortunate are in a way sacrifices to God, as we read in Hebrews (13:16): "Do not neglect to do good and to share what you have, for such sacrifices are pleasing to God." So it is that the words "piety" and "religion" are transferred to works of mercy, and especially to the favors shown to one's parents and country.[12] But adoration (*latria*) suggests the obligation to worship, or the nature of worship (*cultus*), from the fact that we are subjects of him whom we serve—not as one person is called the servant of another because of some debt he might chance to owe him, but because all that we are we owe to him as our creator. So adoration does not mean just any service, but only that by which we are servants of God.[13]

Religion, accordingly, consists in the act by which we worship God by subjecting ourselves to him. This act ought to be in harmony with the one who is worshiped and with the one who does the worshiping. Now he who is worshiped, being a spirit, cannot be contacted by the body but only by the mind. Consequently his adoration consists chiefly in acts of the mind, by which the mind is oriented to God. These are principally acts of the theological virtues; thus Augustine[14] states that God is worshiped by faith, hope and love. To these are added the acts of the gifts which incline us to God, for example, the gifts of wisdom and fear.[15] But because we worshipers of God have bodies and receive our knowledge through bodily senses,

---

[10] St. Augustine, *De civitate Dei* 10.3, CCL 47:275.27-29. See St. Thomas, *Contra gentiles* 3.119.7.

[11] St. Augustine, ibid.

[12] See St. Thomas, *Summa theol.* 2-2.81.1, ad 2; *Contra gentiles* 3.119.8.

[13] See St. Thomas, *Summa theol.* ibid., ad 3; *Contra gentiles* 3.119.10 and 3.120.

[14] St. Augustine, see above, note 1.

[15] On the gifts of the Holy Spirit, see St. Thomas, *Summa theol.* 1-2.68.4.

some actions of the body are also required on our part for the worship of God, not only that we might serve him with our whole being, but also that by these bodily actions we might arouse ourselves and others to acts of the mind directed to God. [16] Thus Augustine says [17]: "Those who pray use their bodily members in a way fitting to suppliants when they genuflect, extend their hands or prostrate themselves on the ground, and perform any other visible action, although their invisible will and their heart's intention is known to God, and he does not need these signs for the revealing of the human spirit, but rather by their means a person stirs himself to pray and to lament his sins more humbly and fervently."

Accordingly all the acts by which we subject ourselves to God, whether they be mental or bodily, are a part of religion. But because those goods that are rendered to our neighbors for the sake of God are rendered to God himself, they clearly belong to the same act of submission in which the worship of religion consists. So, to one who carefully considers the matter, it is clear that every such act is a part of religion. Thus Augustine says [18] that "true sacrifice is every work done that we may adhere to God in holy fellowship." Nevertheless there is a certain order here. First and foremost the acts of the mind directed to God belong to the worship we are talking about. Second, there are the acts of the body performed to stir up and express them, for instance, prostrations, sacrifices and the like. Third, connected with the same worship are all the other acts directed toward our neighbor for the sake of God.

Nevertheless, as magnanimity is a special virtue, [19] though it uses the acts of all the virtues from the special viewpoint of its object, inasmuch as it confers greatness on all virtuous actions, so also religion is a special virtue, taking into account in all virtuous acts the special viewpoint of its object, namely what is owing to God. In this sense it is a part of justice. [20] But those acts are especially allotted to religion that belong to no other virtue, such as prostrations and the like, in which the worship of God secondarily consists.

---

[16] See St. Thomas, *Summa theol.* 2-2.81.7 and 84.2; *Contra gentiles* 3.119.
[17] St. Augustine, *De cura pro mortuis agenda* 5.7, CSEL 41:632.1-7.
[18] See above, note 4.
[19] See St. Thomas, *Summa theol.* 2-2.129.4.
[20] See St. Thomas, *Summa theol.* 2-2.81.4.

From this it is evident that the act of faith belongs materially to religion, just like the acts of the other virtues, and even more so, inasmuch as the act of faith is the primary movement of the mind to God. But it is formally distinct from religion insofar as the viewpoint of its object is different. Besides this, faith is also connected with religion insofar as faith is the cause and source of religion, for no one would choose to show worship to God unless he believed that God is the creator, governor and rewarder of human acts. But religion itself is not a theological virtue, for it has as its subject matter almost all the acts either of faith or of some other virtue, which it offers to God as his due. It has God, however, as its end, for the worship of God is the offering of acts of this kind to God as something owing to him.[21]

The replies to the opposing arguments are evident from what has been said.

ARTICLE THREE

*Is the True Faith Fittingly Called Catholic or Universal?*

*We proceed to the third article as follows:*

It seems that the Christian faith ought not to be called catholic.

*1.* For knowledge ought to be proportionate to the knowable object, for we do not know everything in every possible way. But faith is knowledge of God, who, as Augustine says,[1] is neither universal nor individual. Therefore neither should faith be called universal.

*2.* There can only be individual knowledge of individual things. But we hold by faith the truth of certain individual events, such as the passion and resurrection of Christ, and the like. Therefore faith should not be called universal.

---

[21] See St. Thomas, *Summa theol.* 2-2.81.5.

[1] Perhaps St. Thomas alludes to St. Augustine's *De Trinitate* 7.6.11, CCL 50:261-265. See St. Thomas, *Sent.* 1, d. 19, q. 4, a. 2 and d. 35, q. un., a. 5, sed contra arg. 2, and c; *De veritate* 2.2, ad 4; *Summa theol.* 1.13.9, ad 2 and 14.1, ad 3.

*3.* What is common to many things should not be the basis of our assigning a proper name to any one of them, for we give something a name in order to make it known. But every school or sect proposes its doctrines as something to be universally believed or observed by everyone, and as universally true. Therefore the Christian faith has no special right to be called catholic.

*4.* Idolatry extends to every corner of the earth. But the Christian faith has not yet penetrated all the countries of the world; there are some in foreign lands who do not know the faith of Christ. Therefore the sect of idolatry ought to be called catholic rather than the Christian faith.

*5.* What does not belong to everyone cannot be called universal. But many do not accept the Christian faith. Consequently it cannot fittingly be called catholic or universal.

*On the contrary,* Augustine says[2], "We should cleave to the Christian religion and the communion of its church, which is catholic and is called catholic not only by its members but also by all its enemies."

2. Universal and common seem to be the same. But the Apostle calls the Christian faith the common faith, as is clear in Titus 1:4: "To Titus, my true child, in a common faith," etc. Hence it can fittingly be said to be universal or catholic.

3. What is preached to all ought to be especially called universal. But the Christian faith is preached to everyone, as is evident in Matthew 28:19: "Go therefore and make disciples of all nations," etc. Consequently it should rightly be called catholic or universal.

*Reply:* Like all other knowledge, faith has a twofold subject: that in which it exists, that is, believers themselves, and that about which it is concerned, namely the realities believed; and in both senses the Christian faith can be called catholic.

As regards believers, it is catholic because the Apostle asserts (Romans 3:21) that faith to be true to which "the law and the prophets bear witness." In the time of the prophets, however, different nations followed the cults of various gods; the people of Israel alone gave

[2] St. Augustine, *De vera religione* 7.12, CCL 32:196.12-14.

due worship to the true God. So there did not exist that one world-wide religion that the Holy Spirit foretold through the prophets would be the worship of the true God, and that everyone should adopt. Whence Isaiah says (45:23): "To me every knee shall bow, every tongue shall swear"—a prophecy that was fulfilled by the Christian faith and religion. So it is justly called catholic, for it has been accepted by persons of every condition. Those who have fallen away from this faith and religion—which has been offered to everyone and received by them—to their own beliefs, are not called catholics but heretics, being cut off as it were from its fellowship.

As regards the objects of belief, there is also catholicity in the Christian faith. In ancient times there were various arts and ways of life which provided, or were thought to provide, the human race with different goods. Some theorists placed the good of man solely in goods of the body, either in wealth or honors or pleasures. Others located it solely in goods of the soul, for example in the moral or intellectual virtues. Still others, as Augustine says[3], thought that the gods should be worshiped for the sake of temporal goods in the present life; others for the sake of goods coming after death. Porphyry also held that the imaginative part of the soul—not the whole soul— is cleansed in certain consecrated pagans, and he went on to affirm, as Augustine states,[4] that there has not yet been accepted one religion, offering an all-embracing way of life for the liberation of the human soul.

Now this way of life is the Christian religion, as Augustine declares.[5] It teaches that God should be worshiped not only for the sake of eternal blessings, but also for temporal ones.[6] It instructs the human race not only in spiritual matters but also in the use of goods of the body, and it promises perfect happiness of soul and body. So its laws are said to be universal, giving direction, as they do, to the person's whole life and to everything in any way connected with it.

---

[3] St. Augustine, *De civitate Dei* 6, praef. and c. 1, CCL 47:163.1-164.7 and 164.1-5.
[4] Ibid., 10.9, CCL 47:281.1-282.30.
[5] Ibid., 10.24, CCL 47:297.13-15.
[6] Ibid., 10.14, CCL 47:288.1-29.

It is clear from Boethius' text[7] that he gives both of these reasons for the catholicity [of the faith].

*Replies to Opposing Arguments:*

*Reply to 1.* Though God is neither universal nor individual in himself, he is nonetheless the universal cause and end of all things. So our knowledge of him is in a way universal, extending as it does to everything.

*Reply to 2.* We believe these individual events as universal remedies for the liberation of the whole human race.

*Reply to 3.* Other religions try to claim for themselves what belongs to the Christian faith, but they cannot succeed. So the title "catholic" does not properly belong to them.

*Reply to 4.* Idolatry was not one religion, but it varied among different peoples, because they set up for themselves different gods to be worshiped. Nor was it accepted by all nations, since it was rejected by the worshipers of the true God, as well as by the pagan philosophers, who maintained that these religious rites should be carried out as commanded by law and not as pleasing to the gods, as Augustine says[8], referring to Seneca.

*Reply to 5.* The Christian faith is called catholic or universal not by reason of every individual of each class, but by reason of every class of individuals,[9] for some persons of every condition have accepted it.

ARTICLE FOUR

*Is It an Article of the True Faith that the Father, the Son and the Holy Spirit are Each God, and the Three are One God without Being Separated by Any Inequality?*[1]

*We proceed to the fourth article as follows:*

It seems that it is not an article of the Catholic faith that the Father, Son and Holy Spirit are one God.

---

[7] See above, p. 57.

[8] St. Augustine, *De civitate Dei* 6.10, CCL 47:181.1-183.94. The reference is to Seneca's lost work *De superstitione.*

[9] See St. Thomas, *Expos. in I Tim.* 2, lect. 1, ed. Marietti, n. 62, 2:225; *Summa theol.* 1.19.6, ad 1.

[1] See St. Thomas, *Contra gentiles* 4.6-8.

*1.* For, as Boethius says,[2] if these three are unequal it follows that there are many gods. Now sacred Scripture, which is the source of the Catholic religion, as Augustine states[3], affirms that the Father and Son are unequal. This seems to follow from the words of John 14:28 about the person of the Son: "the Father is greater than I." Hence this is not a belief of the Catholic faith as Boethius claims.

*2.* 1 Corinthians 15:28 states: "When all things are subjected to him," that is, to the Son, "then he himself will also be subjected to him," that is, the Father, "who put all things under himself." So the same conclusion follows as above.

*3.* Prayer is offered only by an inferior to a superior. But the Son prays for us, as Romans 8:34 says: "Christ Jesus...who indeed intercedes for us." The same is true of the Holy Spirit (8:26); "the Spirit himself intercedes for us with sighs too deep for words." Therefore the Son and Holy Spirit are inferior to the Father according to the teaching of the Catholic faith, and so the same conclusion follows.

*4.* In John 17:3, the Son, speaking to the Father, says: "And this is eternal life, that they know you, the only true God, and Jesus Christ whom you have sent." Therefore the Father alone is true God, and not the Son and Holy Spirit. So they appear to be creatures, and the same conclusion follows.

*5.* In 1 Timothy 6:15-16, the Apostle, speaking of the Son, says: "...who (that is, Christ) will be made manifest at the proper time by the blessed and only sovereign, the King of kings and Lord of lords, who alone has immortality and dwells in unapproachable light." So all these titles belong to the Father alone.

*6.* In Mark 13:32 it is said: "But of that day or that hour no one knows, not even the angels in heaven, nor the Son, but only the Father." Therefore the Father's knowledge is greater than the Son's, and so his essence is also greater. The same conclusion follows as above.

*7.* Matthew 20:23 states: "To sit at my right hand and at my left is not mine to grant, but it is for those for whom it has been

---

[2] See above, p. 57.
[3] St. Augustine. *De vera religione* 7.13, CCL 32:196.20-23.

prepared by my Father." Therefore the Son does not have equal power with the Father.

*8.* In Colossians 1:15 it is said of the Son that "he is the first born of all creation." But only things of the same genus can be compared. Therefore the Son is a creature.

*9.* In Ecclesiasticus 24:14 it is said of the person of the divine wisdom: "From eternity, in the beginning, he created me." So the above conclusion follows.

*10.* He who is glorified is less than he who glorifies. But the Son is glorified by the Father, as is clear in John 12:23, 28. Therefore the Son is inferior to the Father.

*11.* The one who sends is greater than the one sent. But the Father sends the Son, as is clear in Galatians 4:4: "God sent forth his Son, born of a woman," etc. He also sends the Holy Spirit according to John 14:26: "...the Counsellor, the Holy Spirit, whom the Father will send in my name." So the Father is greater than the Son and the Holy Spirit. Therefore this teaching of Boethius does not seem to be part of the Catholic faith.

*On the contrary*, it is said in John 1:1, 3: "In the beginning was the Word... and the Word was God... all things were made through him." From this we hold that the Son is eternal, for otherwise he would not exist in the beginning; that he is equal to the Father, for otherwise he would not be God; and that he is not a creature, for otherwise all things would not be made through him.

2. Since the Son is truth, he did not lie about himself. But the Son said he is equal to the Father. Thus it is said in John 5:18: "He also called God his Father, making himself equal with God." Therefore he is equal to the Father.

3. It is said in Philippians 2:6: "He...did not count it robbery to be equal with God." Now it would be robbery if he thought this and it were not true. Therefore he is equal to God.

4. It is said in John 10:30: "I and the Father are one." Again in John 14:10: "I am in the Father and the Father in me." Therefore one is not less than the other.

5. It is said in Romans 9:5: "...of [the patriarchs, and of their race, according to the flesh,] is Christ, who is God over all, blessed forever." Therefore no one is above him, and so he is not less than the Father.

6. It is said in 1 John 5:20: "The Son of God...has given us understanding that we may know the true God, and may be in his true Son. This is the true God and eternal life." Therefore he is not less than the Father.

7. That the Holy Spirit is equal to the Father and true God is evident from the words of Philippians 3:3, according to the Greek text[4]: "We are the circumcision, who serve the Spirit of God." This is taken to be the service of adoration (*latria*), as is clear in the Greek.[5] Now no creature is owed service of this sort according to Deuteronomy 6:13 and Matthew 4:10: "You shall adore the Lord your God and him only shall you serve."[6] Therefore the Holy Spirit is not a creature.

8. The members of Christ cannot be the temple of anyone less than Christ. But our bodies, which are members of Christ in the words of the Apostle,[7] are the temple of the Holy Spirit, as is said in 1 Corinthians 6:19. Therefore the Holy Spirit is not less than Christ, and so neither is he less than the Father. Thus what Boethius calls a teaching of the Catholic faith is true.

*Reply*:   The Arians' position that the divine persons are unequal is not what the Catholic faith professes, but rather a pagan lack of faith. This is clear as follows. According to the pagans all immortal substances were called gods. Among them the Platonists held that there are three primary and principal ones, as Augustine[8] and Macrobius,[9] explain. They are: god the creator of all things, whom they called god the father because everything has come forth from him; a lower substance whom they called the paternal mind or paternal intellect, who contains the ideas of all things and whom they said has been made by god the father. After this they posited a world-soul, as it were the spirit of the life of the whole world. These three substances they called the three main gods and the three principles by which souls are purified.

---

[4] St. Augustine, *De Trinitate* 1.6.13, CCL 50:43.
[5] Ibid.
[6] See *Glossa ordinaria* 5, fol. 16rD.
[7] 1 Cor. 6:15.
[8] St. Augustine, *De civitate Dei* 10.23, CCL 47:296.8-297.21.
[9] Macrobius, *Super somnium Scipionis* 1.2,14-16, p. 482.9-28.

Origen, taking his stand on the teachings of the Platonists, thought that in our faith we should maintain the existence of "three who give witness in heaven" (1 John 5:7), in the way that the Platonists held for three primary substances. So he claimed that the Son is a creature and less than the Father in a book entitled *Peri archon*, or *On Principles*,[10] as Jerome explains in a letter concerning the errors of Origen.[11] And since Origen taught at Alexandria, Arius drank in his error from his writings. For this reason Epiphanius names Origen as the source and father of Arius.[12]

So the position of Arius on the Trinity is as opposed to the Christian and Catholic faith as is the error of the pagans, who in calling creatures gods rendered them the service of divine adoration. The Apostle denounces this in Romans 1:25, saying that "they worshiped and served the creature rather than the Creator," etc.

*Replies to Opposing Arguments:*

*Reply to 1.* As Augustine says,[13] passages in the Scriptures speak of the Father and Son in three ways. Some declare their unity of substance and their equality, for example, "I and the Father are one" (John 10:30). Others reveal the Son as less than the Father because he had the form of a servant, in which respect even he himself made himself less, as is said in Philippians 2:7; "He emptied himself, taking the form of a servant." Still other texts are so worded that he is shown to be neither less than nor equal to the Father, but only that the Son is from the Father, as in John 5:26; "As the Father has life in himself, so he has granted to the Son also to have life." The first authoritative texts are of help to Catholics in defence of the truth. Those that are worded in Scripture in the second and third ways the heretics have adopted to confirm their error, but in vain. For the statements about Christ referring to his human nature should not be applied to his divinity; otherwise it would follow that he died as divine, though in fact this is said of him as human. Neither is it shown that the Son is less than the Father, though the Son is from

---

[10] See Origen, *De principiis* 1.3.5, trans. G. W. Butterworth, pp. 33-34.

[11] St. Jerome, *Ep. 124 ad Avitum*, CSEL 56:97.9.26-98.3.

[12] St. Thomas probably derived this information from a letter of Epiphanius translated by St. Jerome. See St. Jerome, *Ep.* 51. 3, CSEL 54:400.7-10.

[13] St. Augustine, *De Trinitate* 2.1.3, CCL 50:82-84.

the Father, for the Son receives from the Father everything the Father has, as is said in John 16:15 and Matthew 11:27. This allows us to assert an order of origin and not an inequality in the Godhead. Thus the statement "The Father is greater than I" (John 14:28) refers to the Son in his human nature according to Augustine,[14] or, in the words of Hilary,[15] in his divine nature, in such a way that "greater" does not imply inequality. For the Son is not less than the Father, to whom has been given the name above every name, but it indicates the authorship belonging to a principle, inasmuch as the Son has from the Father the name by which the Son is equal to the Father.

·*Reply to 2.*   The Father not only subjected all things to the Son, but he himself made them subject to himself, as is said in Philippians 3:21: "by the power which enables him to subject all things to himself," and this through the divinity, by which he is equal to the Father. Thus, in saying that Christ will be subject to him who subjects all things to himself, the Son is not contrasted with the Father with respect to the divine nature, but rather with respect to the human nature of the Son relative to the Father's divinity, which is common to the whole Trinity. So the faithful themselves are the kingdom of Christ: the kingdom he will hand over to God and the Father (while not dispossessing himself of it), when he will lead the faithful to the vision of the Father: a vision in which his own divinity will also be seen. It will be at that time, when the divine nature will be perfectly known, that he will appear to be subject to the divine nature, especially with respect to his humanity. His subjection, however, is not such that the human nature assumed by Christ is changed into the divine nature, as some heretics claim,[16] but by reason of its being less than the divinity of the Father.

*Reply to 3.*   As Augustine says,[17] "From the fact that the Son prays he is less than the Father; but he grants prayers with the Father from the fact that he is equal to him." In other words, he prays through his human nature and answers prayers through his divine

---

[14]  Ibid., 1.7.14 and 11.22, CCL 50:44-46, 60-61.
[15]  St. Hilary, *De Trinitate* 9.54, CCL 62:431-433.
[16]  The Monophysites. See St. Thomas, *Contra gentiles* 4.35; *Summa theol.* 3.2.1.
[17]  St. Augustine, *De Trinitate* 1.10.21 and 4.8.12, CCL 62:60-61 and 176-177.

nature. But the Holy Spirit is said to intercede for us inasmuch as he makes us petitioners[18] and renders our prayers efficacious.

*Reply to 4.* According to Augustine the statement that there is only one true God should not be understood of the Father alone, but equally of the Father, Son and Holy Spirit. They are called only one true God because there is no true God besides this Trinity. This is how we should understand the text: "that they may know you (that is, the Father) and Jesus Christ whom you have sent" (John 17:3) to be only one true God. No mention is made of the Holy Spirit because, being the bond between the two, we come to know him from both.

*Reply to 5.* As Augustine clearly states,[19] this saying should not be understood of the person of the Father alone, but of the whole Trinity. The whole Trinity is "blessed and only sovereign," etc., and the whole Trinity manifests the Son. If, however, the Apostle had said "whom the blessed Father and only sovereign manifests," this would not indicate that the Son were separate from the Father, any more than it is suggested that the Father is separate from the Son when it is said in Ecclesiasticus 24:8 of the person of the Son, who is the wisdom of God: "I alone have compassed the circuit of heaven." The reason for this is that in anything having to do with the divine essence the Father and Son are entirely one. So what is said of one of them is not denied of the other by an excluding phrase, but only of creatures, which have a different essence.

*Reply to 6.* The Son knows that day and hour not only through his divine nature but also through his human nature, because his soul knows all things. He is said not to know that day, as Augustine says,[20] because he does not make it known to us. Thus he replied to those questioning him about this matter: "It is not for you to know the times or seasons which the Father has fixed by his own authority" (Acts 1:7). In the same way the Apostle said in 1 Corinthians 2:2: "For I decided to know nothing among you except Jesus Christ and him crucified." He did not wish to say more to them because they were unable to grasp it. Or this should be understood of the

---

[18] See St. Thomas, *In Rom.* 8, lect. 5, ed. Marietti, n. 693, 1:124.
[19] St. Augustine, *De Trinitate* 1.6.10, CCL 62:39.
[20] Ibid., 1.12.23, CCL 62:61-62.

Son not as regards his own person as head, but as regards his body which is the church, which, as Jerome says,[21] is ignorant of this matter. But saying that the Father alone knows it indicates that the Son also knows it, according to the principle laid down above.[22]

*Reply to 7.* As Augustine says,[23] the statement "It is not mine to give to you" should be interpreted as follows: It is not within man's power to grant it, giving it to be understood that he grants it because he is God and equal to the Father.

*Reply to 8.* As Augustine states,[24] unintelligent heretics often adduce this text of the Apostle in disparagement of the Son of God, claiming him to be a creature, giving little attention to the meaning of the words. He is said in fact to be first born, not first created, so that he might be believed to be begotten in view of the divine nature he possesses, and first because of his eternity. But even though the Son does not belong to the genus of creatures, nevertheless, as Basil says,[25] he has something in common with them, namely the fact that he receives something from the Father. But he is before creatures in that he possesses by nature what he receives from the Father. For this reason an order can be observed between the generation of the Son and the production of creatures.

*Reply to 9.* That statement and others like it, which we read about the wisdom of God, should be referred either to created wisdom, for example, angelic wisdom, or to Christ himself in his human nature. Thus he is said to be created from the beginning, or in the beginning, as it were predestined from eternity to assume a creature.

*Reply to 10.* As Augustine states,[26] from the fact that the Father glorifies the Son, the Son is not shown to be inferior to the Father; otherwise he would also be inferior to the Holy Spirit, because the Son says of the Holy Spirit: "He shall glorify me" (John 16:14). Glorification (*clarificatio*) does not mean that something takes place in the person of the Son of God, but either in human knowledge (in

---

[21] St. Jerome, *In Evan. sec. Marcum* 13, PL 30:628D.

[22] See St. Thomas, *Summa theol.* 3.10.2, ad 1.

[23] St. Augustine, *De Trinitate* 1.12.25, CCL 62:64.

[24] St. Thomas refers to St. Augustine's *De Trinitate*, but the statement has not been found there.

[25] St. Basil, *Hom. 15, De fide*, n. 2, PG 31:468A.

[26] St. Augustine, *De Trinitate* 2.4.6, CCL 62:86-87.

the sense that manifesting [*clarificare*] means to make our knowledge of him clear), or in the body he assumed, referring to the splendor (*claritatem*) of the Resurrection.

*Reply to 11.* The Son and Holy Spirit are said to be sent by the Father, not that they might be present where previously they were not, but that they might exist in some way in which before they did not, referring to some effect they have in a creature.[27] So the fact that the Son and Holy Spirit are said to be sent by the Father does not reveal an inequality in the Trinity, but the order of origin according to which one person proceeds from another (thus the Father, who does not proceed from another person, is not sent),[28] and also the effectiveness regarding the result the divine person is sent to bring about.

---

[27] St. Thomas, *Summa theol.* 1.43.1.

[28] Ibid., 1.43.4.

# QUESTION FOUR

# ON FACTORS RELATING TO THE CAUSE OF PLURALITY[1]

The next inquiry concerns factors relating to the cause of plurality. Four questions are raised on this subject.

1. Is otherness the cause of plurality?
2. Does a difference of accidents cause a diversity in number?
3. Can two bodies exist, or be thought to exist, in the same place?
4. Does a difference in place have some bearing on a difference in number?

ARTICLE ONE

Is Otherness the Cause of Plurality?

*We proceed to the first article as follows:*

It seems that otherness is not the cause of plurality.

*1.* For, as Boethius says,[2] "From the original constitution of the world, all things whatsoever that have been made seem to have been formed by the nature of numbers. Number was the principal exemplar in the mind of the creator." This agrees with the words of Wisdom 11:21: "But you have arranged all things by measure and number and weight." Therefore plurality or number is first

---

[1] For studies of this article, see bibliography provided by J. F. Wippel, "Thomas Aquinas on the Distinction and Derivation of the Many from the One: a Dialectic between Being and Nonbeing, "*The Review of Metaphysics* 38 (1985), 563 n. 1. Also H. Weidemann, *Metaphysik und Sprache. Eine sprachphilosophische Untersuchung zu Thomas von Aquin und Aristoteles*, pp. 47-61.

[2] Boethius, *De institutione arithmetica* 1. 2, ed. Friedlein, p. 12.14-17.

among created things, and we ought not to look for a created cause of it.

2.   As the *Book on Causes* says,[3] "The first of created things is being." Now the primary division of being is into one and many. So there can be nothing prior to multitude except being and unity. Hence it does not seem to be true that something else is its cause.

3.   Plurality is either found in every genus, according as it is distinguished from the unity that is convertible with being; or it is in the genus of quantity, according as it is distinguished from the unity that is the principle of number.[4] Otherness, however, is in the genus of relation. Now relations are not the causes of quantities; rather, the converse is true. And much less are relations the causes of what is in all genera, because then they would even be the cause of substance. Therefore otherness is in no way the cause of plurality.

4.   Contraries are the causes of contraries; but identity and diversity or otherness are opposites, and so they have opposite causes. Unity, however, is the cause of identity, as is clear in the *Metaphysics*.[5] Consequently plurality or multitude is the cause of diversity or otherness, and so otherness is not the cause of plurality.

5.   The principle of otherness is an accidental difference, for differences of this kind, according to Porphyry,[6] make a thing to be other. But accidental difference, or indeed difference of any kind, is not found in everything in which there is plurality. Certain entities, like simple forms,[7] cannot be the subjects of accidents; others have nothing in common, and so they cannot be said to be different, but rather diverse. The Philosopher explains this in the *Metaphysics*.[8] Hence otherness is not the cause of all plurality.

---

[3] *Liber de causis*, prop. 4, ed. Bardenhewer, p. 166.19.

[4] For the twofold notion of unity, see St. Thomas, *In Metaph.*, 3, lect. 12, n. 501; 5, lect. 8, n. 875 and lect. 10, n. 901; and 10, lect. 3, n. 1981.

[5] Aristotle, *Metaph.* 5. 9 (1018a4-9) and 15 (1021a11).

[6] Porphyry, *Isagoge*, trans. by Boethius (second edition), 4. 1, CSEL 48:240.6-8.

[7] See above, Q. 2, a. 2, 3, p. 40.

[8] Aristotle, *Metaph.* 10. 3 (1054b23-27) and 5. 9 (1018a9-15). Difference is not the same as diversity. Things that are different are composite, being alike in one respect and different in another; for example, a man differs from an ox by the specific difference of rational, while they have in common the genus of animal. Things are diverse by themselves, for example, two beings or two specific differences. See

*On the contrary*, there is the statement of Damascene,[9] that division is the cause of number. Now division consists in diversity or otherness. Therefore diversity or otherness is the source of plurality.

2. Isidore says[10] that number is as it were the signal, that is, the sign, of partition, that is, of division. And so the same conclusion follows.

3. Plurality comes about only through withdrawal from unity. But something withdraws from unity only through division, for something is said to be one from the fact that it is undivided. This is clear in the *Metaphysics*.[11] Therefore division brings about plurality, and so the same conclusion follows.

*Reply*:     As the Philosopher says,[12] something is called many from the fact that it is divisible or actually divided. So whatever causes division ought to be counted as a cause of plurality. Now the cause of division in things that are posterior and composite is different from that in primary and simple things. In posterior and composite items, the formal cause so to speak (in other words, that by reason of which the division is made) is the diversity of simple and prior items. This is clear in the division of quantity. One part of a line is divided from another by having a different position, which is as it were the formal difference of continuous quantity having position. It is also evident in the division of substances. A man is different from an ass by having diverse constitutive differences. But the diversity by which posterior and composite items are divided with respect to prior and simple items presupposes the plurality of prior and simple items. Man and ass have diverse differences because rational and irrational are not one single difference but several. Nor can it always be claimed that this plurality is caused by some diversity of other

---

St. Thomas, *In Metaph*. 10, lect. 4, nn. 2017, 2018; *Contra gentiles* 1.17.7; *Summa theol*. 1.90.1, ad 3. But St. Thomas does not always use these terms in their strict sense.

[9] St. John Damascene, *De fide orthodoxa* 3.5, ed. Buytaert, p. 185.37-38. In fact, Damascene denies that number is the cause of division.

[10] This statement has not been found in the works of Isidore. The word *memeris* in the Decker edition (p. 134.4) is likely a corruption of *merismos* (partition). See St. Thomas, *Sent*. 1, d. 24, q. 1, a. 2, arg. 2, ed. Mandonnet 1:577, note 3.

[11] Aristotle, *Metaph*. 10.3 (1054a23).

[12] Ibid., (1054a22).

prior and simple items, because in that case we would go on to infinity.

Accordingly we must explain the plurality or division of prior and simple items in some other way. They are in fact divided in virtue of themselves. Now it is impossible that being be divided from being insofar as it is being, for nothing is divided from being except non-being. Hence this particular being is only divided from that particular being because this being includes the negation of that being. Thus negative propositions are immediately contained in the primary terms, as though the negation of one were included in the concept of the other. Moreover, the first creature makes up a plurality with its cause, inasmuch as the creature does not measure up to it. In this connection some writers[13] claimed that plurality is caused in a definite order by one primary being. In their view, from one primary being there flows immediately one effect which, along with its cause, make up a plurality. Two effects can now emerge from the first effect: one by reason of [the first effect] itself, the other by reason of its connection with its cause. But we are not forced to affirm this, because one primary item can imitate something in a respect in which another [primary item] fails to do so, and the former can fail [in imitation] in a respect in which the latter achieves imitation. So there can be several first effects, in each of which there is present the negation both of its cause and of the other effect in the same respect, or even in one and the same [effect] by reason of a greater distance [from its cause].

It is clear, then, that the primary reason or source of plurality or division stems from negation and affirmation. So we are to understand that plurality originates according to the following order. Being and non-being are first conceived, and from them are established the primary divided beings, and hence their plurality. So, just as we immediately come upon unity after being, inasmuch as it is undivided, so we at once conceive the plurality of prior and simple items after the division of being and non-being. Now the notion of diversity is a consequence of this plurality, inasmuch as there remains in it the

---

[13] See Avicenna, *Metaph.* 9.4, ed. Van Riet 1:479.94-480.11 and 481.45-484.8. See St. Thomas, *Contra gentiles* 2.42.11; *De potentia* 3.4 and 16; *Summa theol.* 1.47.1; *De substantiis separatis* 10, ed. Leonine 40:D59-D61.

influence of its cause, which is the opposition of being and non-being. For one of several items is called diverse when compared with another because it is not that other. And because a secondary cause produces its effect only through the power of the primary cause,[14] it follows that the plurality of primary items gives rise to division and plurality in secondary and composite ones only insofar as there remains within it the force of the primary opposition, which is between being and non-being, from which it has the nature of diversity. And in this way the diversity of primary items causes the plurality of secondary ones.

So Boethius' statement is true, that otherness is the source of plurality, for otherness is found in some things because diverse items are present in them. Now, although division precedes the plurality of prior items, diversity does not, because division does not require that both of the items divided one from another be a being, since division is present through affirmation and negation. Diversity, however, does require that both items be a being, and so it presupposes plurality. And so diversity can in no way be the cause of the plurality of primary items, unless by diversity is meant division.

Boethius[15] accordingly speaks of the plurality of composite things, as is evident from the fact that he presents a proof concerning things that are diverse in genus, species or number, which has to do only with composite beings, for everything in a genus must be composed of a genus and a difference. Composition, moreover, at least in concept, cannot be avoided by those who claim that the Father and the Son are unequal gods, for they hold them to be alike in being God and to differ in being unequal.

*Replies to Opposing Arguments:*

*Reply to 1.* These statements show that number is prior to other created things, like the elements and other things of this sort, but not prior to other concepts, such as affirmation and negation, division, or other similar notions. However, not every number is prior to everthing created but only the number that is the model of everything,

---

[14] See *Liber de causis*, prop. 1, ed. Bardenhewer, p. 163.3-12.
[15] See above, p. 57.

namely God himself, who, according to Augustine,[16] is the number that gives everything its form.

*Reply to 2.* Plurality, as the word is generally used, immediately follows upon being, but this is not necessarily true of all plurality, and so it is not unfitting that the plurality of what is secondary be caused by the diversity of what is prior.

*Reply to 3.* Like one and many, the same and the diverse are not properties of one genus, but they are, as it were, properties of being as being, and so it is not inappropriate if the diversity of some items be the cause of the plurality of others.

*Reply to 4.* Some plurality precedes all diversity, but diversity does not precede all plurality; rather, some diversity is prior to some plurality. Consequently both statements are true: multitude commonly speaking produces diversity, as the Philosopher says[17]; and diversity brings about plurality in composite beings, as Boethius here declares.[18]

*Reply to 5.* Boethius understands by otherness diversity, which is constituted by differences, whether they be accidental or substantial. Those items, however, which are diverse without being different are primary, but Boethius here makes no mention of them.

ARTICLE TWO

*Does a Difference of Accidents Cause a Diversity in Number?*

*We proceed to the second article as follows:*

It seems that a difference of accidents cannot be the cause of a plurality in number.

*1.* For the Philosopher states[1] that those things are one in number "whose matter is one." It follows that there is plurality in number where there is plurality of matter. Therefore it is not a difference of accidents, but rather a diversity of matter that causes numerical diversity.

---

[16] St. Augustine, *De natura boni* 3, CSEL 25 (pt. 2), 856.10-24.
[17] Aristotle, *Metaph.* 5.9 (1018a9-11).
[18] See above, p. 57.

[1] Aristotle, *Metaph.* 5. 6 (1016b31-33).

2. The Philosopher says[2] that the cause of the substance and of the unity in things is the same. But accidents are not the cause of the substance in individuals and therefore neither of their unity. So they cannot be the cause of numerical plurality.

3. Because all accidents are forms, they are by their very nature communicable and universal. But nothing like this can be the principle of individuation for something else. Hence accidents are not the principle of individuation. But some things are numerically diverse inasmuch as they are divided as individuals. Consequently accidents cannot be the source of numerical diversity.

4. Just as things differing in genus or species in the genus of substance differ substantially and not only accidentally, so also things that differ in number. But some things are said to be different in genus or species through what is in the genus of substance. Similarly, therefore, things are said to differ in number through what is in the genus of substance and not through accidents.

5. If a cause is taken away, so too is its effect. Now every accident can be removed from its subject, either in fact or in thought. Consequently, if an accident were the principle of identity and diversity in number, it could happen that in fact or in thought the same things were sometimes one and sometimes diverse in number.

6. What is posterior is never the cause of what is prior. But among all accidents quantity holds the first place, as Boethius says.[3] Among quantities, moreover, number is by nature prior because it is more simple and abstract. Consequently no other accident can be the principle of numerical plurality.

*On the contrary*, there is the statement of Porphyry,[4] that an individual is produced by an assembling of accidents which cannot be found in any other individual. But the principle of individuation is the principle of numerical diversity. Accidents, therefore, are the principle of plurality in number.

2. We find nothing in the individual except form, matter and accidents. Now diversity of form is not the cause of diversity in

---

[2] Ibid., 10. 1 (1052a33).

[3] Boethius, *In categorias Aristotelis* 2. PL 64: 201D-202D.

[4] Porphyry, *Isagoge*, trans. by Boethius (second edition). 3. 2, CSEL 48: 234.14-16.

number, but rather diversity in species, as is clear in the *Metaphysics*.[5] Diversity in genus is the result of the diversity of matter, for the Philosopher states[6] that things differ "in genus if they do not have their matter in common and are not generated out of each other." Therefore nothing can bring about diversity in number except diversity of accidents.

3. What is found in common in several things different in species is not the cause of diversity in number, because the division of a genus into species precedes the division of the species into individuals. But matter is found in common in things diverse in species, because the same matter is the subject of contrary forms; otherwise things having contrary forms would not be changed into each other. Therefore matter is not the principle of diversity in number, and neither is form, as has been proved. So it follows that accidents are the cause of this diversity.

4. In the genus of substance we find nothing but genus and difference, but the individuals of one species differ neither in genus nor by reason of substantial differences; therefore they differ only by reason of accidental differences.

*Reply*:   In order to clarify this question and those raised in the text of Boethius we must see what causes the three kinds of diversity mentioned in the text.[7] There are only three items in a composite individual in the genus of substance: matter, form and the composite of the two. It is from among these, then, that we must find the causes of each of these diversities. We should know that diversity in genus is reducible to diversity of matter, while diversity in species is reducible to diversity of form, but diversity in number is reducible partly to diversity of matter and partly to diversity of accidents.

Now because a genus is the beginning of knowledge, being the first part of a definition, while matter in itself is unknown, it follows that diversity in genus cannot be taken from matter as it is considered in itself, but only in the way in which it is knowable. Now it is in fact knowable in two ways. In one way by analogy or proportion,

[5]  Aristotle, *Metaph.* 10. 9 (1058b1).
[6]  Ibid., 10. 3 (1054b27-29).
[7]  See above; p. 57.

as the *Physics* says.[8] For example, we may say that matter is that
which has the same relation to natural things as wood has to a bed.
In another way matter is known through form, through which it has
actual existence, for everything is known inasmuch as it is actual
and not inasmuch as it is potential, as is said in the *Metaphysics*.[9]

Accordingly diversity in genus is derived from matter in two ways.
First, because of a different relation to matter. In this way the primary
genera of things are distinguished with reference to matter. What is
in the genus of substance is related to matter as to one of its parts.
What is in the genus of quantity does not have matter as one of its
components, but it is related to matter as its measure. Quality in turn
is related to it as its disposition. Through these two genera all the
other genera receive different relationships to matter. Matter itself
is a part of substance, and it gives to substance its nature as a subject,
because of which it bears a relation to accidents. In a second way
diversity in genus is derived from matter inasmuch as matter is
perfected through form. Matter is pure potentiality and God is pure
actuality, and for matter to be brought into the actuality that is form
is nothing but its sharing, though imperfectly, a likeness of the
primary actuality. Thus what is composed of matter and form is in
between pure potentiality and pure actuality.

Matter, however, does not uniformly receive an equal resemblance
to the primary actuality; by some things it is received imperfectly,
by others more perfectly. Some things share the divine likeness only
to the extent that they subsist, some to the extent that they live, some
to the extent that they know, and still others to the extent that they
understand.[10] Now the likeness itself of the primary actuality existing
in any matter is its form. But a form of this kind causes only existence
in some things, in others existence and life, and so with other forms,
each of which remains one and the same, for a more perfect likeness
possesses everything a less perfect likeness does, and more besides.
There is something common, accordingly, in both likenesses, which
in one is the ground of imperfection and in another the ground of
perfection, as matter is the basis of both actuality and privation. Thus

---

[8]  Aristotle, *Physics* 1. 7 (191a7-12).
[9]  Aristotle, *Metaph.* 10. 9 (1051a29-32).
[10]  See St. Thomas, *Contra gentiles* 3.20.

matter, along with this common factor, still functions as matter with respect to the perfection and imperfection mentioned above.

A genus, accordingly, is derived from this material factor, whereas differences are taken from the above-mentioned perfection and imperfection.[11] For example, we take the genus "living body" from the common material condition of possessing life, while we derive the difference "sentient" from an added perfection, and the difference "insentient" from an imperfection. In this way the diversity of these material factors results in a diversity in genus, for example, the diversity between animal and plant. For this reason matter is called the principle of diversity in genus, and for the same reason form is the principle of diversity in species, for the differences that determine species are taken from the above-mentioned formal principles, which are related to the aforesaid material factors, from which genera are derived, as form to matter.

It should be borne in mind, however, that because the material factor which is the basis of the genus includes both matter and form, the logician considers the genus only on its formal side, with the consequence that his definitions are called formal. The natural philosopher, on the other hand, takes both aspects of the genus into consideration.[12] Thus it can happen that something is in a genus from the logician's point of view which is not in a genus from the perspective of the natural philosopher. For it is possible that the resemblance to the primary actuality that something receives in matter of a particular kind something else might receive without matter, and something else again might receive it in matter of an entirely different kind. For example, it is evident that stone comes to subsist in matter potential to existence; the sun comes to subsist through matter potential to place and not to existence; and an angel subsists without any matter whatsoever. So the logician, finding in all of these the source from which he derived a genus, places all of them in the same genus of substance. The natural philosopher and metaphysician, however,

---

[11] See St. Thomas, *De ente et essentia* 2, ed. Leonine 43:372.169-183 and 195-201; *In Metaph.* 5, lect. 22, n. 1123.

[12] For the difference between the logical and natural consideration of a genus, see Q. 6, a. 3, ed. Decker, p. 222.13-18, trans. Maurer, p. 86. See St. Thomas, *Sent.* 1, d. 19, q. 5, a. 2, ad 1; *Summa theol.* 1.88.2, ad 4; *In Metaph.* 10, lect. 12, n. 2142.

who take into account all the principles of a thing, assert that they are in different genera, for they do not find them sharing the same matter. This agrees with the statements of the *Metaphysics*,[13] that the perishable and the imperishable differ in genus, and that things are in the same genus which have their matter in common and are generated out of each other.

It is clear, then, how matter causes diversity in genus and form diversity in species. Diversity in individuals of the same species should be understood as follows.[14] As the Philosopher says,[15] just as the parts of a genus and species are matter and form, so the parts of an individual are *this* matter and *this* form. It follows that just as diversity of matter or form taken absolutely causes diversity in genus and species, so *this* form and *this* matter bring about diversity in number. Now no form as such is individual of itself. I say "as such" because of the rational soul, which in a sense is of itself an individual substance,[16] but not insofar as it is a form. For any form that can be received in something as in matter or in a subject can be predicated by the mind of many things, which is opposed to the nature of an individual substance. Consequently form is rendered individual through being received in matter. But because matter in itself lacks all differentiation, it can individuate the received form only insofar as it itself bears some distinguishable mark. So form is individuated by being received in matter, but only as it is received in *this* particular matter, determined to this place and this time. Matter, however, is divisible only through quantity. Thus the Philosopher says[17] that if quantity were taken away, substance would remain indivisible. Accordingly matter is made to be *this* and designated owing to the fact that it is subject to dimensions.

Now dimensions can be understood in two ways. In one way inasmuch as they are determinate, and by this I mean that they have a definite measurement and shape. In this sense, as complete beings,

---

[13] Aristotle, *Metaph.* 10. 10 (1058b26-29 and 1059a9), 10. 3 (1054b27-29).

[14] See St. Thomas, *De principio individuationis*, ed. Perrier 1: 573-577. This treatise is of doubtful authenticity. See J. A. Weisheipl, *Friar Thomas d'Aquino*, pp. 403-404.

[15] Aristotle, *Metaph.* 7.10 (1035b27-31).

[16] See St. Thomas, *Quaestiones de anima* 1.1.

[17] Aristotle, *Physics* 1. 2 (185b16).

they are located in the genus of quantity. Now when dimensions are understood in this way they cannot be the principle of individuation, because there is often a variation in such determination of dimensions in the same individual, and thus it would follow that the individual would not always remain the same in number. In another way dimensions can be taken as indeterminate, simply as having the nature of dimensions, though they can never *exist* without some determination, any more than the nature of color can exist without being definitely white or black. Taken in this way dimensions are located in the genus of quantity as something incomplete. It is through these indeterminate dimensions that matter is made to be this designated matter (*haec materia signata*), thus rendering the form individual. In this way matter causes diversity of number in the same species.[18]

It is clear, then, that matter taken in itself is the principle of neither specific nor numerical diversity. But it is the principle of generic diversity inasmuch as it underlies a common form, and so likewise it is the principle of numerical diversity as underlying indeterminate dimensions. Because these dimensions belong to the genus of accidents, diversity in number is sometimes reduced to the diversity of matter and sometimes to diversity of accidents, and this because of the dimensions mentioned above. But other accidents are not the principle of individuation, though they are the cause of our knowing the distinction between individuals. In this sense individuation can also be ascribed to the other accidents.

*Replies to Opposing Arguments;*

*Reply to 1.* The Philosopher's statement that those things are one in number whose matter is one is to be understood as referring to designated matter, which is the subject of dimensions; otherwise we would have to say that all generable and corruptible things are one in number because their matter is one.

---

[18] St. Thomas took the notion of indeterminate dimensions from Averroes. See Averroes, *De substantia orbis* 1, fol. 3M-4E. See St. Thomas, *Sent.* 2, d. 3, q. 1, a. 4 and 4, d. 12, q. 1, a. 1, ad tert, quaest. and ad 3. After the period of this commentary he spoke only of determinate dimensions, or simply of dimensive quantity, as the principle of individuation. See *Contra gentiles* 4.63.65; *Summa theol.* 1.76.6, ad 2 and 3.77.2; *De potentia* 9.1, 2, ad 1. On this question see M.-D. Roland Gosselin, *Le "De ente et essentia" de s. Thomas d'Aquin*, pp. 104-126; L. Elders, *Faith and Science*, pp. 69-81.

*Reply to 2.* Because dimensions are accidents, they cannot by themselves be the source of the unity of an individual substance. But matter, as the subject of these dimensions, is understood to be the principle of such unity and plurality.

*Reply to 3.* By definition the individual is undivided in itself and divided from other things by the last of all divisions.[19] Now among accidents quantity alone has of itself the special characteristic of division. So dimensions of themselves have a certain character of being individual with reference to a definite position, position being a quantitative difference. Thus a dimension is individual on two scores: because of its subject, just like any other accident; and also because of itself, insofar as it has position. Owing to its position, even if we abstract from sensible matter we can imagine a particular line and a particular circle. So it rightly belongs to matter to individuate all other forms because it is the subject of that form which of itself has the trait of being individual. Indeed even determinate dimensions themselves, which are grounded in the already completed subject, are in a sense individuated by matter that has been rendered individual by the indeterminate dimensions that we conceive beforehand in matter.

*Reply to 4.* Things differing in number in the genus of substance differ not only in their accidents but also in their form and matter. But if you ask why their form is different, no other reason can be given except that it exists in a different designated matter. Neither can any other explanation be found why this matter is divided from that except quantity. Consequently matter, as subject to dimension, is understood to be the principle of this diversity.

*Reply to 5.* That argument is based on complete accidents, which are consequent upon the existence of form in matter, not on indeterminate dimensions, which are conceived of before the reception of form in matter, for without these the individual cannot be understood, just as it is unintelligible without form.

*Reply to 6.* Number, formally speaking, is prior to continuous quantity, but materially speaking continuous quantity is prior, for

[19] See St. Thomas, *Summa theol.* 1.29.4; *In Metaph.* 10, lect. 10, n. 2133. In the logical tree of Porphyry, genera are divided into species and lastly species into individuals. See Porphyry, *Isagoge*, trans. by Boethius (second edition), 3. 1-12. CSEL 48:199-236.

number is the result of the division of the continuum, as the *Physics* says.[20] In this way the division of matter according to dimensions causes diversity in number.

As for arguments *on the contrary*, it is clear from what has been said to what extent they are to be granted and to what extent they arrive at erroneous conclusions.

ARTICLE THREE

*Can Two Bodies Exist, or Be Thought to Exist, in the Same Place?*[1]

*We proceed to the third article as follows:*

It seems that two bodies can be thought to exist in the same place.

*1.* For every proposition seems to be intelligible whose subject does not include the opposite of the predicate, for an intelligible proposition does not contain contradictory concepts. Now the proposition "Two bodies are in the same place" is not of this sort; otherwise it could never miraculously happen that two bodies were in the same place. This is clearly false regarding our Lord's body, which came forth from the closed womb of the Virgin[2] and entered the company of the disciples while the doors were shut.[3] For God cannot make an affirmation and negation to be true at the same time, as Augustine asserts.[4] Therefore one can at least mentally conceive of two bodies being in the same place.

---

[20] Aristotle, *Physics* 8. 8 (263a23-26).

[1] See St. Thomas, *Sent.* 4, d. 44, q. 2, a. 2, qu. 2 and 3; *In Phys.* 4, lect. 13, n. 1; *Quodlibet* 1, q. 10, a. 21 and 22; *Summa theol.* 3.54.1, ad 1 and 57.4, ad 2; *Super Evangelium S. Ioannis* 20, lect. 4, ed. Cai, p. 469; *Ad 1 Cor.* 15, lect. 6, ed. Cai 2: 422, n. 983.

[2] See St. Thomas, *Summa theol.* 3.28.2.

[3] See John 20:19, 26.

[4] St. Augustine, *Contra Faustum* 26. 5, CSEL 25 (pt. 1), 732.22-25, 733.4-7 and 11-17.

*2.* Glorified bodies do not lose the nature of corporeality, but only the nature of fleshiness. But, as many claim,[5] the gift of subtlety removes from them the condition of being incapable of existing in the same place. This condition, therefore, is not a result of the nature of corporeality, but rather of fleshiness or a kind of density. Hence it is not always impossible for two bodies to occupy the same place.

*3.* Augustine[6] speaks of light as holding first place in bodies. But light is simultaneously in the same place as air. Therefore two bodies can occupy the same place at the same time.

*4.* Every species of fire is a body. But light, as the Philosopher says,[7] is a kind of fire. Therefore light is a body, and so the same conclusion follows.

*5.* In glowing iron the fire and the iron exist together. But both are bodies. Therefore it is possible for two bodies to exist in the same place at the same time.

*6.* Elements are not eliminated in a compound; otherwise the compound would not conform to the movement of the dominant element. But all four elements are bodies, and they exist simultaneously in every part of the compound. Therefore two bodies can exist in the same place.

*7.* The fact that two bodies are not in the same place cannot be true of bodies because of matter, for place is not due to matter in itself, nor for the same reason is it because of form; nor is it because of dimension, since dimensions do not fill place, as is clear from the fact that some writers[8] called the place occupied solely by dimensions a vacuum. Therefore this is true of a body only because of subsequent accidents which are not common to all bodies and which can be separated from them. So it seems that two bodies can occupy the same place.

---

[5] This was the position of St. Bonaventure, *Sent.* 4, d. 49, pt. 2, sect. 2, a. 3, q. 1, ed. Quaracchi 4: 1028-1029. See St. Albert, *Sent.* 4, d. 44, a. 23, ed. Borgnet 30:574-575.

[6] St. Augustine, *De Genesim ad litteram* 1. 9, CSEL 28 (sect. 3, pt. 2), 13.25; *De libero arbitrio* 3.5.16, CCL 29 (pt.2²), 284-285.

[7] Aristotle, *Topics* 5. 5 (134b28-30).

[8] See St. Thomas, *Sent.* 4, d. 44, q. 2, a. 2, qu. 2, sol.; *In Phys.* 4. 8, lect. 13, n. 1, ed. Leonine 2:190a.

*8.* According to astronomers who follow Ptolemy,[9] the six planetary bodies move in epicycles,[10] which are circles intersecting the eccentric spheres of the planets. The body of the planet, accordingly, must at some time arrive at the place of intersection. Now it cannot be said that there is a vacuum there, for nature abhors a vacuum; nor that the substance of the spheres is divisible, so that it might be thought to give way to the planetary body when it arrives there, as air gives way to a stone or to some other body, since the heavens are "most strong, as if they were of molten brass," according to Job 37:18. Hence the planetary body must be simultaneously in the same place as the body of its sphere. So Boethius' statement here[11] is false, that two bodies never occupy the same place.

*On the contrary,* if two bodies can be in the same place, with equal reason any number of bodies can occupy the same place.[12] But a body, however large, can be divided into small bodies of any quantity and in any number. It will follow, then, that the largest body will be contained in the smallest place, which seems absurd.

2. There cannot be several straight lines between two given points. Now this impossibility would result if two bodies were in the same place. For, given two points in two opposite locations, there will be two given straight lines between them in the two bodies in place. It cannot be said that between these two points there is no line at all, nor that one body in place has a line between the points but the other does not, nor that there is one line between two points of place apart from the bodies in place, because then that line would not exist in a subject. Therefore it is impossible for two bodies to exist in the same place.

3. It is proved in geometry that two circles are tangent at only one point. But if we postulate two bodies in the same place, it will

---

[9] See Ptolemy, *Almagest* 3.3, ed. Heibert, pp. 216.22-217.2 and 219.13-16. See also St. Thomas, *In De caelo et mundo* 2, lect. 17, n. 5, ed. Leonine 3:188a; *In Metaph.* 13, lect. 10, n. 2567-2569.

[10] See John of Sacrobosco, *De spera* 4, ed. Thorndike, p. 114.

[11] See above, p. 57.

[12] See Aristotle, *Physics* 4.8 (216b10).

follow that two given circles in them are completely tangent. Therefore it is impossible for two bodies to be in the same place.

4. If several things are the same as one and the same thing, they are the same as each other. But the dimension of the place and of the thing in place must be the same, because there cannot be dimensions without a subject. Therefore, if two bodies are in the same place, it follows that the dimensions of both bodies are the same as the dimensions of the place, and consequently that they are the same as each other, which is impossible.

*Reply*: Regarding all the things that surround us, which are conceded to be bodies, we perceive with our senses that when one body arrives at a place another body is forced out of that place. So it is clear from experience that two bodies of this kind cannot occupy the same place. Some writers,[13] however, claim that two of these bodies are not prevented from being [in the same place] at the same time because of the fact that they are bodies, or because of anything connected with the nature of bodiness as such, for then it would follow that two bodies under all circumstances would be prevented from existing [in the same place] at the same time. Rather, they assert that this cannot occur owing to the fleshiness (*corpulentia*) of these bodies. But whatever they might mean by fleshiness—whether the density or impurity or corruptibility of some bodies, or even a special nature added to the general nature of bodiness—it cannot be the reason this cannot happen.

A body, in fact, is related to place in two ways. One way is by being located in this or that definite place. This relationship is a consequence of the specific nature of this or that body. For example, heavy bodies, owing to the nature of heaviness, are below, whereas light bodies, owing to the nature of lightness, are above. The other relation obtains when a body is said to be in place purely and simply. A body has this relation from the very nature of corporeality, not because of some property added to the body. For a body is in place from the fact that it is commensurate with that place, and this is because it is measured by dimensions equal and similar to the dimensions of the place. Dimensions, moreover, belong to every body

---

[13] See above, note 5.

from the very nature of corporeality. Now the question whether several bodies can or cannot occupy the same place does not concern a definite place, but place absolutely. Hence the cause standing in the way of simultaneity in place concerns the very nature of corporeality, which gives to every body as such its natural property of being in place. And if the last sphere is not in place, the reason is simply that there can be nothing outside of it, and not that it lacks the aforesaid natural property.

Others[14] grant without qualification that no two bodies can occupy the same place, and as the reason for this they offer mathematical principles, which ought to be taken into account (*salvari*) in all natural bodies, according to the treatise *On the Heavens and the Earth*.[15] This, however, does not seem appropriate, because mathematical objects cannot be in place in the strict sense but only metaphorically, as is said in the treatise *On Generation*.[16] Thus the reason for this impossibility should not be based on mathematical principles, but rather on the principles of natural bodies, to which place is properly ascribed. Further, mathematical arguments are not sufficiently conclusive in this matter. For although mathematics are to be taken into account in natural bodies, nevertheless natural bodies add sensible matter to mathematical objects, and because of this addition it is possible to explain something in the natural sciences which could not be advanced as an explanation in mathematics. Thus, in mathematics the only reason that can be offered for the diversity of two particular lines is their position. If diversity of position is eliminated, there are no longer several mathematical lines, nor likewise several surfaces or bodies. Therefore there cannot be several mathematical bodies occupying the same place at the same time, and the same holds good for lines and surfaces.[17]

Accordingly we should adopt Avicenna's way of thinking in his *Physics*, in the treatise on place.[18] He explains the above-mentioned

---

[14] See St. Thomas, *In Phys.* 4, lect. 13, n. 1, ed. Leonine 2:189a-190b. St. Albert, *In Phys.* 4, tr. 2, c. 8, ed. Borgnet 3:297a. St. Bonaventure, *Sent.* 4, d. 49, p. 2, sect. 2, a. 3, q. 1, ed. Quaracchi 4:1028b-1029a.

[15] Aristotle, *De caelo* 3, 1 (299a13-15).

[16] Aristotle, *De gen. et corr.* 1, 6 (323a1-3).

[17] See St. Bonaventure, note 14 above.

[18] Avicenna, *Sufficientia* 2.7, fol. 28vb54-29rb5.

impossibility by natural principles, giving as its cause the nature itself of corporeality. The only cause of this impossibility, he says, is that to which it belongs primarily and of itself to be in place, for this is what naturally fills place. Now it is only accidental for form to be in place, though some forms are the principle by which a body is determined to some special place. Matter likewise, taken in itself, is not in place, for in this way it is conceived apart from all the other genera, as the *Metaphysics* says. [19] Consequently matter must prevent this inasmuch as it is the subject of that through which it is primarily related to place, and it is related to place by being subject to dimensions.

Thus several bodies are prevented from being in the same place by the nature of matter inasmuch as it is subject to dimensions. For there must be many bodies in which the form of corporeality is divided, and it is divided only by the division of matter. Since matter is divided only because of dimensions, which by definition have position, this particular matter cannot be distinct from that particular matter unless they have different positions. But this is not the case when two bodies are supposed to occupy the same place, for then those two bodies would be in fact one body, which is impossible. Consequently, since matter is subject to dimensions in all bodies, any two bodies are prevented from occupying the same place by the very nature of corporeality.

*Replies to Opposing Arguments:*

*Reply to 1.* A proposition can be said to be unintelligible in two ways. In one way on the part of the knower who lacks understanding. An example is the proposition: "In the three divine persons there is one essence." A proposition of this kind need not imply contradiction. In another way the unintelligibility may be on the side of the proposition itself, and this for two reasons. First, it may absolutely imply a contradiction; for example, "What is rational is irrational," and the like. Not even by a miracle can such propositions be made true. Other propositions contain a contradiction in a certain sense, as for example, "A dead man returns to life." This includes a contradiction when the man is understood to return to life by his own power, for the assertion that he is dead implies that he lacks every vital principle.

---

[19] Aristotle. *Metaph.* 7.3 (1029a20).

Propositions of this sort can be made to be true by a miracle worked by a higher power. The same is true in the present case. There is no natural cause available to diversity two bodies in the same place, but the divine power can preserve their distinction even though they have the same position. Thus it can happen miraculously that two bodies occupy the same place.

*Reply to 2.* Whatever this fleshiness may be that is said to be removed from glorified bodies, nevertheless it is clear that corporeality will never be removed from them, and so neither will the cause that by nature prevents one of them from being in the same place at the same time as another body. Only by a miracle is it possible for them to occupy the same place at the same time with other bodies.

*Reply to 3.* Light is not a body but a kind of quality, as both Damascene[20] and Avicenna assert.[21] Augustine,[22] however, calls light fire, as is evident from the fact that he differentiates light from air, water and earth.

*Reply to 4.* The three species of fire spoken of by the Philosopher[23] are to be understood as follows. By light is meant fire as it exists in its own matter, even though it might be granted, as some claim,[24] that fire emits no light in its own sphere. For it is not the nature of light to be luminous, but by participating in it other things are made to glow. The same is true of fire: although it does not emit light in its own matter, nevertheless by participating in it other things become luminous. By flame is meant fire existing in aerial matter, and by live coals fire in terrestrial matter. In watery substance fire cannot retain its strength to the point that it has the nature of fire, because water has all the qualities opposed to fire.

*Reply to 5.* In glowing iron there are not two bodies; rather, there is one body in the species of iron, along with certain properties of fire.

*Reply to 6.* Although elements are said to remain in a compound with their substantial forms, they are not said to be actually several

---

[20] St. John Damascene, *De fide orthodoxa* 1. 8, ed. Buytaert, p. 34.121.

[21] Avicenna, *De anima* 3.1, ed. Van Riet 1:173.46-47. See St. Thomas, *Sent.* 2, d. 13, q. 1, a. 3; *Summa theol.* 1.67.2.

[22] This statement has not been found in Augustine's writings.

[23] Aristotle, *Topics* 5.5 (134b28-30).

[24] Moses Maimonides, *Guide of the Perplexed* 2.31.

bodies. Otherwise no compound would be truly one entity. But it is actually one and potentially many. The opinion of the Commentator[25] seems to be more probable. Rejecting the position of Avicenna,[26] he claims that the forms of the elements do not remain in a compound, nor are they completely destroyed, but from them there arises an intermediate form inasmuch as they admit of degrees. But it is unheard of that substantial forms should permit of degrees. So it seems that his statement should be understood as follows. The forms of the elements allow of degrees not in themselves but inasmuch as they remain virtually in the elementary qualities as in their proper instruments. Thus it can be said that the forms no longer exist in themselves, but only inasmuch as they exist virtually in their qualities, out of which there arises one intermediate quality.[27]

*Reply to 7.* Although dimensions of themselves could not fill a place, nevertheless a natural body has the property of filling a place from the fact that its matter is understood to be the subject of dimensions.

*Reply to 8.* Ptolemy's opinion about epicycles and eccentric spheres does not seem to be in harmony with Aristotle's principles of natural philosophy, and so his opinion is not acceptable to Aristotle's followers.[28] If it is adopted, however, there will be no necessity for two bodies to exist in the same place. For according to the followers of that opinion there are three different kinds of substances in the heavenly bodies: the substance of the stars, which is luminous; the substance of the spheres, which is transparent and solid but not divisible; and another substance which is between the spheres and which is divisible and condensable like air, though it is indestructible.[29] Owing to this substance they avoid the necessity of holding that the substance of the spheres is divided, or that two bodies exist in the same place.

---

[25] Averroes, *In De caelo et mundo* 3, com. 67, fol. 231-232.

[26] Ibid.

[27] In his later writings St. Thomas abandoned this interpretation of Averroes. See *Quaestiones de anima* 9, ad 10.

[28] See St. Thomas, *In De caelo et mundo* 2, lect. 17, ed. Leonine 3:186-188, n. 2, 3, 5.

[29] On this third kind of substance, see St. Thomas, *In Metaph.* 12, lect. 10, n. 2569.

ARTICLE FOUR

*Does a Difference in Place Have Some Bearing on a Difference in Number?*

*We proceed to the fourth article as follows:*

It seems that a difference in place has nothing to do with diversity in number.

*1.* For the cause of numerical diversity is within the things themselves that differ in number. But place is outside of things in place. Therefore the cause of numerical diversity cannot come from diversity of places.

*2.* A thing is complete in its being only when it is distinct from other things. But place comes after a thing has complete being. Thus motion to a place is the motion of something perfected in its substance, as the *Physics* says.[1] Therefore we cannot obtain from place a cause of differentiation of bodies in place.

*3.* Distinction in number does not change regarding distinct things. But an unchanging effect is not the result of a changing cause. Therefore, since place changes regarding the thing in place, diversity in place cannot be the cause of diversity in number.

*4.* Remove the cause and you remove the effect. But, as was said before,[2] distinction in place is sometimes removed from two bodies by a miracle, and yet they remain distinct in number. Therefore distinction in place does not cause diversity in number.

*5.* Diversity in number is found not only in bodies but also in incorporeal substances. But difference of places cannot cause their diversity in number, for incorporeal substances are not in place, as Boethius himself says.[3] Therefore difference in place cannot always be cited as the cause of diversity in number, as he himself seems to say.

---

[1] Aristotle, *Physics* 8. 7 (260b33) and (261a17-21).
[2] See above, Q. 4, a. 3, Reply to 1 and 2, pp. 105-106.
[3] Boethius, *De hebdomadibus*, p. 40.25-26.

*On the contrary* is the fact that things differing in number are diversified by accidents. But the diversity of no accident is so inextricably bound up with diversity in number as is diversity of place. Therefore diversity of place seems to be most responsible for diversity in number.

2. The specific difference of places goes hand in hand with the specific difference of bodies, as is evident in the case of heavy and light bodies. Therefore the numerical difference of places also inseparably goes along with the numerical difference of bodies, and so the same conclusion follows.

3. As time measures motion, so place measures a body. But motion is divided numerically according to time, as the *Physics* says[4]. Therefore a body is also divided numerically according to place.

*Reply*: As is clear from what was said above,[5] diversity in number is caused by the division of matter existing under dimensions. Matter itself, as existing under dimensions, also prevents two bodies from being in the same place, inasmuch as each of the two bodies must have matter with a distinct position. So it is evident that diversity in number has the same cause as the necessity of different bodies having different places. Accordingly the difference of places, taken in itself, is an indication of diversity in number, as we also said above[6] concerning other accidents, except the first indeterminate dimensions. But if we regard difference of place from the viewpoint of its cause, then difference of place is clearly the cause of diversity in number. So Boethius here determines[7] that it is undoubtedly true that difference of accidents brings about diversity in number, disregarding all other factors in the difference of places, for none of the other accidents which outwardly appear complete is so close to the cause of diversity in number as difference of places.

*Replies to Opposing Arguments:*

*Reply to 1,2,3.* These arguments conclude that difference of place is not in itself the cause of the diversity of individuals, but

---

[4] Aristotle, *Physics* 6. 4 (234b21, 235a10-13). The text of St. Thomas erroneously refers to book 5.

[5] See above, Q. 4, a. 2 and 3, pp. 97, 104-105.

[6] See above, Q. 4, a. 2, p. 98.

[7] See above, p. 57.

this does not deny the fact that the cause of the difference of places in the cause of diversity in number.

*Reply to 4.* All the effects of secondary causes are more dependent on God than they are on the secondary causes themselves.[8] So even without the secondary causes he can by a miracle bring about the effects he wishes.[9]

*Reply to 5.* The diversity in number of incoporeal substances is a consequence of their difference in species, except in the case of the rational soul, whose numerical diversity follows upon the division of matter disposed to receive it.[10] Boethius, however, is here speaking of diversity in number within the same species.

*In answer to the arguments to the contrary,* I reply to the first that difference of accidents other than indeterminate dimensions is not the cause that brings about diversity in number; rather, it is said to bring it about as a sign indicating the diversity. Taken in this sense, difference of place plays the greatest role because it is the sign most closely related to diversity in number.

2. The specific difference of places is an indication of the specific difference of bodies, but it is not its cause.

3. Although the division of time is caused by the division of motion, difference of time is likewise not the cause, but the sign, of the difference of motion. The same is true of place with regard to bodies.

---

[8] See *Liber de causis*, prop. 1, ed. Bardenhewer, p. 163.3.

[9] See St. Thomas, *Contra gentiles* 3.99 and 4.65.3; *Summa theol.* 1.105.6 and 3.77.1.

[10] See St. Thomas, *Summa theol.* 1.50.4; *Contra gentiles* 2.93; *De ente et essentia* 5, ed. Leonine 43:376.79-89 and 378.51-379.71; *De spiritualibus creaturis* 8.

# BIBLIOGRAPHY

## A. WORKS OF THOMAS AQUINAS CITED

Complete Editions of the Works of Thomas Aquinas:
————. Opera omnia. Ed. Leonine. Rome: Typographia Polyglotta, 1882-.
————. Opera omnia. 34 vols. Paris: Vivès, 1871-1880.
————. Opera omnia. 25 vols. Parma: Fiaccadori, 1852-1873.

Anthologies:
An Aquinas Reader. Ed. M. T. Clark. New York: Doubleday, 1972.
Basic Writings of St. Thomas Aquinas. Ed. A. C. Pegis. 2 vols. New York: Random House, 1945.
Introduction to St. Thomas Aquinas. Ed. A. C. Pegis. New York: Random House, A Modern Library Book, 1948.
The Pocket Aquinas. Ed. V. J. Bourke. New York: Washington Square Press, 1965.
St. Thomas Aquinas: Theological Texts. Ed. T. Gilby. London: Oxford University Press, 1955.

Individual Works of Thomas Aquinas:
De ente et essentia. Ed. Leonine 43. Rome, 1976.
Le "De ente et essentia" de s. Thomas d'Aquin. Ed. M.-D. Roland-Gosselin. Paris: J. Vrin, 1948. Trans.: On Being and Essence. A. A. Maurer. 2nd ed. Toronto: Pontifical Institute of Mediaeval Studies, 1968. Aquinas On Being and Essence. J. Bobik. Notre Dame: University Press, 1965.
De mixtione elementorum. In Opuscula philosophica 1. Ed. J. Perrier. Paris: Lethielleux, 1949. Trans.: "On the Combining of the Elements." V. R. Larkin. Isis 51 (1960), 67-72.
De potentia Dei, Quaestiones disputatae. Ed. R. Spiazzi et al. Rome-Turin: Marietti, 1949. Trans.: On the Power of God. English Dominican Father (L. Shapcote). 3 vols. London: Burns, Oates and Washbourne, 1932-1934.
De principio individuationis. In Opuscula philosophica 1. Ed. J. Perrier. Paris: Lethielleux, 1947.
De rationibus fidei ad Cantorem Antiochenum. Ed. Leonine 40. Rome, 1969.

*De spiritualibus creaturis.* Ed. L. Keeler. Rome: Gregorianum, 1946. Trans.: *On Spiritual Creatures.* M. C. Fitzpatrick and J. J. Wellmuth. Milwaukee: Marquette, 1951.

*De substantiis separatis.* Ed. Leonine 40. Rome, 1958. Trans.: *Treatise on Separate Substances.* F. J. Lescoe. West Hartford, CT 1959.

*De veritate, Quaestiones disputatae.* Leonine 22. Rome, 1970-1974. Trans.: *On Truth.* R. M. Mulligan, J. V. McGlynn, and R. W. Schmidt. 3 vols. Chicago: Regnery, 1952-1954.

*Expositio in duodecim libros Metaphysicorum Aristotelis.* Ed. M.-R. Cathala and R. Spiazzi. Turin-Rome: Marietti, 1950. Trans.: *Commentary on the Metaphysics of Aristotle.* J. P. Rowan. 2 vols. Chicago: Regnery, 1964.

*Expositio in libros Aristotelis De Caelo et Mundo.* Ed. Leonine 3. Rome, 1886.

*Expositio in libros Aristotelis Meteorologicorum.* Ed. Leonine 3. Rome, 1886.

*Expositio in libros Peri hermenias.* Ed. Leonine 1. Rome, 1882. Trans.: *Aristotle on Interpretation. Commentary by St. Thomas and Cajetan.* J. T. Oesterle. Milwaukee: Marquette, 1962.

*Expositio in libros Posteriorum Analyticorum.* Ed. Leonine 1. Rome, 1882. Trans.: *Commentary on the Posterior Analytics of Aristotle.* F. R. Larcher. Albany, N. Y.: Magi Books, 1970.

*Expositio in octo libros Physicorum Aristotelis.* Ed. Leonine 2. Rome, 1884. Trans.: *Commentary on Aristotle's Physics.* R. J. Blackwell et al. New Haven: Yale, 1963.

*Expositio in symbolum apostolorum, scilicet "Credo in Deum."* In *Opuscula theologica 2.* Ed. R. Spiazzi. Rome: Marietti, 1954.

*Expositio super librum Boethii De Trinitate.* Ed. B. Decker. Leiden: E. J. Brill, 1955. Repr. with corrections, 1959. Trans.: *The Trinity and Unicity of the Intellect.* Sister R. E. Brennan. St. Louis: Herder, 1946. *On Searching into God* (Q. 2). V. White. Oxford: Blackfriars, 1947. *The Division and Methods of the Sciences* (Qq. 5-6). A. Maurer. 4th ed. Toronto: Pontifical Institute of Mediaeval Studies, 1986.

*Lectura super epistolas S. Pauli.* Ed. P. R. Cai. 2 vols. Turin-Rome: Marietti, 1953.

*Lectura super Evangelium S. Iohannis.* Ed. P. R. Cai. 5th ed. Turin-Rome: Marietti, 1952. Trans.: *Commentary on the Gospel of St. John* (Part 1). J. A. Weisheipl and F. R. Larcher. Albany, NY: Magi Books, 1980.

*Quaestiones de anima.* Ed. J. H. Robb. Toronto: Pontifical Institute of Mediaeval Studies, 1968. Trans.: *Questions on the Soul.* J. H. Robb. Milwaukee: Marquette, 1984.

*Quaestiones quodlibetales.* Ed. R. Spiazzi. Turin-Rome: Marietti, 1956. Trans.: *Quodlibetal Questions 1 and 2.* S. Edwards. Toronto: Pontifical Institute of Mediaeval Studies, 1983.

*Responsio ad magistrum Ioannem de Vercellis de 43 articulis*. Ed. Leonine 42. Rome, 1979.

*Scriptum super libros Sententiarum*. Ed. P. Mandonnet and M. F. Moos. 4 vols. Paris: Lethielleux, 1929-1947.

*Sententia libri De anima*. Ed. Leonine 45.1. Rome, 1984. Trans.: *Aristotle's De Anima with the Commentary of St. Thomas Aquinas*. K. Foster and S. Humphries. New Haven: Yale, 1951.

*Sententia libri Ethicorum Aristotelis*. Ed. Leonine 47. Rome, 1969. Trans.: *Commentary on the Nicomachean Ethics*. C. I. Litzinger. 2 vols. Chicago: Regnery, 1964.

*Summa contra gentiles*. Ed. Leonine 13-15. Rome, 1918-1930. Trans.: *On the Truth of the Catholic Faith*. A. C. Pegis, J. F. Anderson, V. J. Bourke, and C. O'Neil. 5 vols. New York: Doubleday, 1955-1957.

*Summa theologiae*. Ed. Leonine 4-12. Rome, 1888-1906.

*Summa theologiae*. Ed. and trans. T. Gilby. 60 vols. New York-London: McGraw-Hill, 1964-1969.


B.   ANCIENT AND MEDIEVAL WRITERS CITED OTHER THAN THOMAS AQUINAS


Albert the Great. *Commentarii in librum Sententiarum*. In *Opera omnia* 30. Ed. A. Borgnet. Paris: Vivès, 1894.

———. *Commentarii B. Dionysii Areopagitae*. In *Opera omnia* 14. Ed. A. Borgnet. Paris: Vivès, 1892.

Ambrose. *De fide*. PL 16: 549-726.

———. *De spiritu sancto*. PL 16: 731-850.

Anselm. *Proslogion*. In *Opera omnia* 1. Ed. F. S. Schmitt. Edinburgh: T. Nelson, 1946-1961.

Aratus, *Phaenomena*. Ed. E. Maass. Berlin, 1893.

Aristotle. *Opera graece ex recensione I. Bekkeri*. Ed. Academia Regia Borussica. Berlin, 1831-1870.

———. *Selected Works*. Trans. Hippocrates G. Apostle and Lloyd P. Gerson. Grinnell, Iowa: The Peripatetic Press, 1982.

———. *The Works of Aristotle*. Ed. W. D. Ross. 12 vols. London: Oxford University Press, 1908-1952.

Augustine. *Confessiones*. Ed. L. Verheijen. CCL 27. Turnhout: Brepols, 1981.

———. *Contra duas epistolas Pelagianorum*. PL 44: 549-638.

———. *Contra Faustum*. Ed. J. Zycha. CSEL 25. Vienna: Tempsky, 1891.

———. *De civitate Dei*. Ed. B. Bombart and A. Kalb. CCL 47-48. Turnhout: Brepols, 1955.

———. *De cura pro mortuis gerenda*. Ed. J. Zycha. CSEL 41. Vienna: Tempsky, 1900.

———. *De doctrina christiana*. Ed. J. Martin. CCL 32. Turnhout: Brepols, 1962.

———. *De Genesi ad litteram*. Ed. J. Zycha. CSEL 28. Vienna: Tempsky, 1894.

———. *De libero arbitrio*. Ed. W. M. Green. CCL 29. Turnhout: Brepols, 1970.

———. *De magistro*. Ed. K.-D. Daur. CCL 29. Turnhout: Brepols, 1970.

———. *De natura boni*. Ed. J. Zycha. CSEL 25. Vienna. Tempsky, 1892.

———. *De praedestinatione sanctorum*. PL 44: 959-992.

———. *De Trinitate*. Ed. W. J. Mountain. CCL 50-50a. Turnhout: Brepols, 1968.

———. *De utilitate credendi*. Ed. J. Zycha, CSEL 25. Vienna: Tempsky, 1891.

———. *De vera religione*. Ed. K.-D. Daur. CCL 32. Turnhout: Brepols, 1962.

———. *Enarrationes in Psalmos*. Ed. D. E. Dekkers and J. Fraipont. CCL 38-40. Turnhout: Brepols, 1956.

———. *Enchiridion*. Ed. E. Evans. CCL 46. Turnhout: Brepols, 1969.

———. *Epistula 28 ad Hieronymum*. Ed. A. Goldbacher. CSEL 34. Vienna: Tempsky, 1895.

———. *Soliloquia*. PL 32: 869-904.

Pseudo-Augustine. *Hypomnesticon contra Pelagianos et Coelestianos*. PL 45: 1611-1664.

Averroes. *Aristotelis opera cum Averrois commentariis*. Venice: Juntas, 1562-1574. 11 vols. Repr. Frankfurt: Minerva, 1962.

———. *Commentarium magnum in Aristotelis de Anima libros*. Ed. F. S. Crawford. Cambridge, Mass.: The Mediaeval Academy of America, 1953.

Avicenna. *Liber de anima seu sextus de naturalibus*. Ed. S. Van Riet. 3 vols. Louvain-Leiden: E. J. Brill, 1968, 1972, 1980.

———. *Liber de philosophia prima sive scientia divina*. Ed. S. Van Riet. 2 vols. Louvain-Leiden: E. J. Brill, 1977, 1980.

———. *Opera*. Venice, 1508. Repr. Frankfurt: Minerva, 1962.

Basil. *Homiliae*. PG 31: 163-618.

Boethius. *De differentiis topicis*. PL 64: 1173-1216.

———. *De institutione arithmetica*. Ed. G. Friedlein. Leipzig, 1867. Repr. Frankfurt: Minerva, 1966.

———. *In categorias Aristotelis*. PL 64: 159-294.

———. *In Isagogen Porphyrii commenta*. Ed. S. Brandt. CSEL 48. Vienna: Tempsky, 1906.

————. *The Theological Tractates and the Consolation of Philosophy.* Ed. and trans. H. F. Stewart, E. K. Rand and S. J. Tester. The Loeb Classical Library, Cambridge, Mass.: Harvard University Press, 1973.

Bonaventure. *Collationes in Hexaëmeron.* In *Opera omnia* 5. Ed. Collegium S. Bonaventurae, ad Claras Aquas (Quaracchi) 1882-1902.

————. *Commentaria in iv libros Sententiarum* In *Opera omnia* 1-4.

————. *Quaestiones disputatae de scientia Christi.* In *Opera omnia* 5.

Cicero. *De inventione.* Ed. E. Stroebel. Leipzig, 1915.

————. *De officiis.* Ed. C. Atzert. Leipzig, 1932.

————. *Tusculanae disputationes.* Ed. C. F. W. Müller. Leipzig, 1898.

Damascene, John. *De fide orthodoxa.* Ed. E. M. Buytaert. St. Bonaventure, New York: Franciscan Institute, 1955.

Dionysius, Pseudo-Areopagite. *Opera.* PG 3.

————. *Dionysiaca. Recueil donnant l'ensemble des traduction latines des ouvrages attribués au Denys de l'Aréopage.* Ed. Ph. Chevallier. 2 vols. Paris: Desclée, 1937.

Epimenides. In *The Pre-Socratic Philosophers. A Companion to Diels, Fragmente der Vorsokratiker.* Ed. K. Freeman. Oxford: Basil Blackwell, 1946.

Epiphanius. *Epistola ad Iohannem episcopum Ierosolymorum.* See Jerome. *Epistola 51.* CSEL 54. Vienna: Tempsky, 1910.

Eustratius. *In Ethicam Nicomacheam.* In *The Greek Commentaries on the Nicomachean Ethics of Aristotle in the Latin Translation of Robert Grossesteste* 1. Ed. H. P. F. Mercken Leiden: E. J. Brill, 1973.

*Glossa ordinaria. Biblia sacra cum glossa ordinaria...et postilla Nicolai Lyrani,* vols. 1, 3, 6. Paris, 1590. *Bibliorum sacrorum cum glossa ordinaria et Nicolai Lyrani expositionibus,* vols. 4, 5. Lyons, 1545.

*Glossa interlinearis.* In *Biblia sacra,* as above.

Gregory the Great. *Homiliae in Evangelium.* PL 76: 1075-1312.

————. *Moralia in Job.* Ed. M. Adriaen. CCL 143AB. Turnhout: Brepols, 1979-1985.

Hilary of Poitiers. *De Trinitate.* Ed. P. Smulders. CCL 62-62A. Turnhout: Brepols, 1979-1980.

Horace. *De arte poetica. Horatius, Carmina.* Ed. F. Vollmer. Leipzig, 1907.

Hugh of St. Victor. *De sacramentis christianae fidei.* Ed. C. H. Buttimer. Washington, D. C., 1939.

Jerome. *Commentaria in Danielem.* Ed. F. Glorie. CCL 75A. Turnhout: Brepols, 1964.

————. *Commentaria in Esaiam.* Ed. M. Adriaen. CCL 73, 73A. Turnhout: Brepols, 1963.

————. *Commentaria in Prophetas Minores. In Osee Prophetam.* Ed. M. Adriaen. CCL 76. Turnhout: Brepols, 1969.

————. *Commentarius in evangelium secundum Marcum*. PL 30: 589-614.

————. *Contra Rufinum*. Ed. P. Lardet. CCL 79. Turnhout: Brepols, 1982.

————. *Epistulae*. Ed. I. Hilberg. CSEL 54 and 56. Vienna: Tempsky, 1910 and 1918.

————. *Liber psalmorum*. PL 28.

John of Sacrobosco. *Tractatus de spera*. In *The Sphere of Sacrobosco and Its Commentators*. Ed. Lynn Thorndike. Chicago: University of Chicago Press, 1949.

*Liber de causis*. Ed. O. Bardenhewer. In *Die pseudo-aristotelische Schrift über das reine Gute, bekannt unter dem Namen Liber de causis*. Freiburg, 1882.

Macrobius. *Commentarium in somnium Scipionis*. Ed. F. Eyssenhardt. Leipzig, 1893.

Maimonides. *The Guide of the Perplexed*. Trans. Shlomo Pines. Chicago: University of Chicago Press, 1963.

Menander. *Menandri quae supersunt. Thais*. Ed. A. Koerte. Leipzig, 1953.

Origen. *On First Principles (De principiis)*. Trans. G. W. Butterworth. New York: Harper and Row, 1966.

Peter Lombard. *Sententiae in iv libris distinctae*. Ed. tertia. Editiones collegii S. Bonaventurae Ad Claras Aquas. 2 vols. Rome: Grottaferrata, 1971, 1981.

————. *In epistolam ad Romanos*. PL 191: 1301-1534.

Plotinus. *Enneads*. Edd. P. Henry and H. R. Schwyzer. Oxford: Clarendon Press, 1977. Trans.: *The Enneads*. S. MacKenna. 2nd rev. ed. B. S. Page. London: Faber and Faber, 1956.

Porphyry. *Isagoge*. Latin trans. Boethius. In *Isagogen Porphyrii commenta* Ed. G. Schepss. CSEL 48. Vienna: Tempsky, 1906.

————. *Isagoge, translatio Boethii*. In *Aristoteles latinus* 1, pt. 6-7. Ed. L. Minio-Paluello. Bruges-Paris: Desclée de Brouwer, 1966.

————. *Isagoge*. Trans. E. W. Warren. Toronto: Pontifical Institute of Mediaeval Studies, 1975.

Ptolemy. *Syntaxis mathematica*. Ed. I. L. Heibert. Leipzig, 1898.

Richard of St. Victor. *De Trinitate*. PL 196: 887-992.

Seneca. *Epistulae*. Ed. O. Hense. Leipzig, 1914.

Vigilius Thapsensis. *De unitate Trinitatis*. PL 42: 1207-1212.

William of Auvergne. *De anima*. In *Opera omnia*, II, supp., pp. 65-228. Orleans-Paris, 1674. Repr. Frankfurt: Minerva, 1963.

William of Tocco. *Vita S. Thomae Aquinatis*, c. 3. n. 15. In *Acta sanctorum* 7: 661. Paris-Rome, 1865.

## C. Modern Authors Cited

Bobik, Joseph. "La doctrine de s. Thomas sur l'individuation des substances corporelles." *Revue philosophique de Louvain* 51 (1953), 5-41.

———. "Dimensions in the Individuation of Bodily Substances." *Philosophical Studies* 4 (1954), 60-79.

Bourke, Vernon J. *Augustine's Quest of Wisdom: Life and philosophy of the Bishop of Hippo.* Milwaukee: Bruce, 1945.

Chenu, Marie-Dominique. "La date du commentaire de s. Thomas sur le *De Trinitate* de Boèce." *Revue des sciences philosophiques et théologiques* 30 (1941-1942), 432-434.

———. *Faith and Theology.* Trans. D. Hickey. New York: Macmillan, 1968.

———. *Is Theology a Science?* Trans. A. H. N. Green-Armytage. New York: Hawthorn Books, 1959.

———. *La théologie comme science au XIIIᵉ siècle.* 3rd ed. Paris: J. Vrin, 1957.

———. *Toward Understanding Saint Thomas.* Trans. A.-M. Landry and D. Hughes. Chicago: Regnery Press, 1964.

Congar, Yves. *Thomas d'Aquin: sa vision de théologie et de l'Église.* London: Variorum Reprints, 1984.

———. "Theology's Tasks after Vatican II." In *Theology of Renewal* 1: 47-65. Ed. L. K. Shook. Montreal: Palm Publishers, 1968.

———. *A History of Theology.* Trans. H. Guthrie. Garden City, NY, 1968.

Decker, Bruno. "Corrigenda et Addenda à l'édition du 'In Boethium de Trinitate' de s. Thomas d'Aquin." *Scriptorium* 13 (1959) 81-82.

Degl' Innocenti, Umberto. "Il pensiero di san Tommaso sul principio d'individuazione," *Divus Thomas* (Piacenza) 45 (1942), 35-81.

*Documents of Vatican II.* Ed. W. M. Abbott. New York: Guild Press, 1966.

Elders, Leo. *Faith and Science. An Introduction to St. Thomas' Expositio in Boethii De Trinitate.* Rome: Herder, 1974.

Ernst, Cornelius. "Theological Methodology." In *Sacramentum Mundi* 6: 218-224, ed. K. Rahner. New York: Herder and Herder, 1970.

Gils, Pierre-Marie. "L'édition Decker du 'In Boethium de Trinitate' et les autographes de s. Thomas d'Aquin." *Scriptorium* 10 (1956), 111-120.

———. [Notes on reprint of Decker's edition, Leiden, 1959]. *Bulletin thomiste* 11 (1960-1961), 41-44, n. 54.

Gilson, Etienne. *The Christian Philosophy of Saint Augustine.* Trans. L. E. M. Lynch. New York: Random House, 1960.

———. *The Christian Philosophy of St. Thomas Aquinas.* Trans. L. K. Shook. New York: Random House, 1956.

————. *Elements of Christian Philosophy*. Garden City, NY: Doubleday, 1960.

————. *History of Christian Philosophy in the Middle Ages*. New York: Random House, 1955.

————. "The Intelligence in the Service of Christ the King." In *A Gilson Reader*, ed. A. C. Pegis, pp. 31-48. Garden City, NY: Doubleday, 1957.

————. *The Philosopher and Theology*. Trans. C. Gilson. New York: Random House, 1962.

————. "Pourquoi saint Thomas a critiqué saint Augustin." *Archives d'histoire doctrinale et littéraire du moyen âge* 1 (1926) 5-127.

————. *The Spirit of Mediaeval Philosophy*. New York: Scribner's, 1940.

Grabmann, Martin, *Die theologische Erkenntnis- und Einleitungslehre des hl. Thomas von Aquin auf Grund seiner Schrift "In Boethium de Trinitate," im Zusammenhang der Scholastik des 13. und beginnenden 14. Jahrhunderts dargestellt*. Freiburg in Schweiz: Paulusverlag, 1948.

Gracia, Jorge J. E. *Introduction to the Problem of Individuation in the Early Middle Ages*. Washington, DC: The Catholic University of America Press, 1984.

Gutierrez, Gustavo. *A Theology of Liberation: History, Politics and Salvation*. Maryknoll: Orbis, 1973.

John Paul II. "Method and Doctrine of St. Thomas in Dialogue with Modern Culture." In *Two Lectures on St. Thomas Aquinas*. Niagara, NY: Niagara University, no date.

Jolivet, Roland. *Dieu soleil des esprits*. Paris: Desclée de Brouwer, 1934.

Klinger, Inghert. *Das Prinzip der Individuation bei Thomas von Aquin*. Munsterschwarzach: Vier-Turme, 1964.

Lloyd, A. C. "Neoplatonic Logic and Aristotelian Logic, I and II." *Phronesis* 1 (1955) 58-72, 146-160.

Lubac, Henri de. *Exégèse médiévale. Les quatre sens de l'Écriture*. 2² partie, vol. 4. Paris: Aubier, 1964.

Mair, John. "The Text of the *Opuscula Sacra*." In *Boethius: His Life, Thought and Influence*, ed. Margaret Gibson, pp. 206-213. Oxford: Blackwell, 1981.

Maritain, Jacques. *Distingush to Unite: or, The Degrees of Knowledge*. Trans. G. B. Phelan et al. New York: G. Scribner, 1959.

Moeller, Charles. "Renewal of the Doctrine of Man." In *Theology of Renewal* 2: 420-463, ed. L. K. Shook. Montreal: Palm Publishers, 1968.

Neumann, Siegfried. *Gegenstand und Methode der theoretischen Wissenschaften nach Thomas von Aquin auf Grund der Expositio super librum Boethii De Trinitate. Beiträge zur Geschichte der Philosophie* und Theologie des Mittelalters. Texte und Untersuchungen 41, vol. 2. Münster: Aschendorf, 1965.

Owens, Joseph. "The Aristotelian Conception of the Sciences." *International Philosophical Quarterly* 4 (1964), 200-216. Repr. in *Aristotle. The Collected Papers of Joseph Owens*, ed. John R. Catan, pp. 23-34. Albany: State University of New York, 1981.

————. *Human Destiny. Some Problems for Catholic Philosophy.* Washington, DC : The Catholic University of America Press, 1985.

————. "A Note on Aquinas, *In Boeth. de Trin.*, 2, 2 ad 1ᵐ." *The New Scholasticism* 59 (1985), 102-108.

————. "Thomas Aquinas: Dimensive Quantity as Individuating Principle." *Mediaeval Studies* 50 (1988).

*The Oxford Dictionary of the Christian Church.* Ed. F. L. Cross. 2nd ed. rev. F. L. Cross and E. A. Livingstone. Oxford: University Press, 1978.

Pegis, Anton C. *St. Thomas and Philosophy.* The Aquinas Lecture, Milwaukee: Marquette University Press, 1964.

————. "Penitus Manet Ignotum." *Mediaeval Studies* 27 (1965), 212-226.

Pelikan, Jaroslav. *The Christian Tradition. A History of the Development of Doctrine* 1. Chicago and London: University of Chicago Press, 1971.

Peter, Carl J. "A Shift to the Human Subject in Roman Catholic Theology." *Communio* 6.1 (1979), 56-72.

Quinn, John F. *The Historical Constitution of St. Bonaventure's Philosophy.* Toronto: Pontifical Institute of Mediaeval Studies, 1973.

Rahner, Karl. *Grundsätzliche Überlegungen zur Anthropologie und Protologie im Rahmen der Theologie. Mysterium Salutis* 2. *Die Heilgeschichte vor Christus.* Einsiedeln: Benzinger, 1967.

————. "Theology." In *Sacramentum Mundi* 6: 233-246. New York: Herder and Herder, 1970.

————. "Theology and Anthropology," In *Theological Investigations* 9: 28-45. Trans. G. Harrison. New York: Herder and Herder, 1972.

Shook, Laurence K. *Etienne Gilson.* Toronto: Pontifical Institute of Mediaeval Studies, 1984.

Smalley, Beryl. *The Study of the Bible in the Middle Ages.* 3rd ed. Oxford: Blackwell, 1983.

Van Ackeren, Gerald F. *Sacra Doctrina. The Subject of the First Question of the Summa Theologica of Saint Thomas Aquinas.* Rome: Catholic Book Agency, 1952.

Vansteenkiste, C. "Un testo di San Tommaso in edizione critica." *Angelicum* 33 (1956), 437-442.

Wallace, William. *Causality and Scientific Explanation*. 2 vols. Ann Arbor: University of Michigan Press, 1972, 1974.

Weidemann, Hermann. *Metaphysik und Sprache. Eine sprachphilosophische Untersuchung zu Thomas von Aquin und Aristoteles*. Freiburg-Munich: Karl Alber, 1975.

Weisheipl, James A. "The Meaning of *Sacra Doctrina* in *Summa Theologiae* I, q. 1." *The Thomist* 38 (1974), 49-80.

———. *Friar Thomas d'Aquino. His Life, Thought and Work*. Garden City, NY, 1974. 2nd ed. Washington, DC: The Catholic University of America Press, 1983.

Winiewicz, David. "A Note on *alteritas* and Numerical Diversity in St. Thomas Aquinas." *Dialogue* 16 (1977), 693-707.

Wippel, John F. *Metaphysical Themes in Thomas Aquinas*. Washington, DC: The Catholic University of America Press, 1984.

———. "Thomas Aquinas on the Distinction and Derivation of the Many from the One: a Dialectic between Being and Nonbeing." *The Review of Metaphysics* 38 (1985), 563-590.

Wolfson, Harry A. *Philo. Foundations of Religious Philosophy in Judaism, Christianity, and Islam*. 2 vols. Cambridge, MA.: Harvard University Press, 1947.

# Index of Names

Albert, St., xiii, 101 n, 104 n.
Ambrose, St., xii, 5 n, 31, 35, 36, 45.
Ammonius Saccas, xxiv.
Anselm, St., 25, 29.
Aratus, 47.
Arians, 57, 58, 60, 61, 80.
Aristotle (the Philosopher), *passim*.
Arius, xxiv, xxvii n, 58 n, 81.
Augustine, St., *passim*.
Averroes (the Commentator), xxxiv, 98 n, 107.
Avicenna, xvi, xvii, xxvi, 16, 21, 25, 90 n, 104, 106, 107.

Basil, St., 47, 84.
Bobik, J., xxxiv n.
Boethius, *passim*.
Bonaventure, St., xv n, xvi, xxxvii, 26 n, 101 n, 104 n.
Bourke, V., xvi n.

Chenu, M.-D., vii n, ix n.
Cicero, xix, 45, 66, 70, 71.
Congar, Y., ix n, xxxvi, xxxvii

Damascene, St. John, 20, 25, 40, 89, 106.
Decker, B., xxxvii.
Degli' Innocenti, U., xxxiv n.
Dionysius (Pseudo-Areopagite), xiii, 7, 15, 19, 22, 24, 36, 50, 52, 53, 64.

Elders, L., vii n, xv n, xxxiv n, xxxv n, 13 n, 26 n, 36 n, 98 n.
Epimenides, 46, 47 n.
Epiphanius, 81.
Ernst, C., xii n.
Eustratius, 9 n.

Felician, 37.

Gils, P.-M., xxxviii
Gilson, E., ix n, xii n, xvii, xviii n, xxiv n, xxxii n, xxxv n, 13 n, 22 n.
Grabmann, M., ix n, xiii n, 13 n, 26 n.
Gracia, J. J. E., xxiv n, xxix n, xxx m.
Gregory, St., 14, 23, 36, 47, 53.
Grosseteste, Robert, 9 n.
Gutierrez, G., x n.

Hilary, St., xii, 6, 37, 38, 39, 82.
Horace, 11.
Hugh of St. Victor, x, 65.

Isidore of Seville, St., 89.

Jerome, St., 36, 41 n, 45-47, 48 n, 50, 81, 84.
John of Sacrobosco, 102 n.
John Paul II, xxxvii n.
Jolivet, R., xvi n.

# Index of Biblical Citations

Scriptural citations follow the Douay /
Vulgate version of the Bible

## OLD TESTAMENT

## NEW TESTAMENT

# Index of Subjects